Counselling at Work

Counselling at Work

Edited by

Lynn Macwhinnie

Association for Counselling at Work 1998
A Division of the British Association for Counselling

First published in Great Britain by the
Association for Counselling at Work 1993-1997
in *Counselling at Work* (ISSN: 1351:007X)

© Association for Counselling at Work 1998

The Association for Counselling at Work is a
Division of the British Association for Counselling

Association for Counselling at Work
Eastlands Court, St Peters Road,
Rugby CV21 3QP, Warwickshire
Tel: 01788 335617 Fax: 01788 335618

British Association for Counselling
1, Regent Place, Rugby CV21 2PJ
Warwickshire
Tel: 01788 578328

0870 443 5252

British Library Cataloguing in Publication Data.
A catalogue record for this book is available from the British Library

ISBN: 0 946181 70 5

Design by DesignWrite Productions
Printed and bound by the Russell Press Ltd, Nottingham, UK

Foreword

The Boots Company has a long history of providing comprehensive employee care services. Many other organizations are now providing varying degrees of counselling support to employees, making the whole area of counselling in the workplace a dynamic growth area.

There are many facets to counselling in an organizational setting, making it a much more complex area than counselling in, for example, private practice. Managing an internal or external counselling service, delivering staff training in the use of counselling skills, providing employee counselling or maintaining the boundaries of confidentiality must all be interpreted and enacted within the ethics and values inherent in the provision of counselling.

As workplace counselling is still a relatively new initiative in the UK, the information and resources for developing and implementing an appropriate counselling service have not been widely available.

The Association for Counselling at Work (ACW) has, for several years, been steadily addressing these issues through its network of members working in organizations across the sectors. Their experience has been consistently and effectively reflected in the ACW journal *Counselling at Work* which is relevant to any organization committed to enhancing interpersonal communication or in developing an ethical workplace counselling service.

This anthology provides a welcome synthesis of articles which have stood the test of time in the changing world of workplace counselling.

Andy Smith
Director of Personnel (Group)

THE BOOTS COMPANY

Preface

This book represents a cross-section of articles which have been published in the ACW journal *Counselling at Work* from its inception in 1993 to the end of 1997. The current and previous ACW Executive committees were the selection panel for the articles chosen for this anthology: their aim has been to ensure a continuing relevance for the broadest readership within this field. Any subject omissions are more than likely due to the fact that someone has yet to 'volunteer' to write an article on a particular topic for the journal!

The contributors to the journal have included managers, HR professionals, organizational consultants, trainers, EAP providers and of course, counsellors. Their direct experience of the different levels of application of counselling continues to influence, by example, the development of the counselling at work profession in its widest context. The anthology provides an overview of their collective expertise giving the reader a range of practical information which is applicable to their own working environment.

The anthology is divided into four sections: A Context for Workplace Counselling; Change Management; Dynamics of Relationships; and Creating Success. While an article may be found within a particular section, it will inevitably have themes and issues which resonate with other sections.

Acknowledgments

I would like to thank all the contributors to this book and, in particular, Andrew Rankin for his initial ideas in helping to define a structure for the anthology.

On a more general note, I would also like to express my thanks and appreciation to all those who have contributed articles, reviews, reports and news items to the past 19 issues of the journal.

Lynn Macwhinnie
Editor, *Counselling at Work* journal
April 1998

Contents

I — A Context for Workplace Counselling

II — Change Management

III — Dynamics of Relationships

IV — Creating Success

Contributors

Andrea Adams was author of *Bullying at Work* (Virago). She died in 1995, and the Andrea Adams Trust National Helpline has been established for people experiencing workplace bullying.

Mike Bagshaw is a consultant specializing in management training, coaching and conflict mediation. He was formerly Director of Training & Development, Coutts Consulting Group.

Andrew Bull has a private counselling and supervision practice, having formerly been a lecturer in counselling at the University of Birmingham.

Gregg Butler PhD left BNFL in 1996, and is now a consultant. He is a member of the Radioactive Waste Management Advisory Committee and Chairman of Westlakes Scientific Consulting Ltd.

Catherine Carroll MSc is a BAC-accredited counsellor, who formerly worked in-house for Shell International. She is a counsellor, supervisor, consultant and trainer on the Diploma in Counselling at Work, University of Bristol.

Michael Carroll PhD is a chartered counselling psychologist, Fellow of BAC, and a BAC-recognized supervisor, working as a counsellor, supervisor and trainer, specializing in employee well-being.

Romey Chapman is an independent counsellor and supervisor, specializing in bereavement and loss.

Susan Clayton is a chartered psychologist, and partner at the Executive Transformation Company.

David Charles-Edwards is a management consultant specializing in leadership, team building and counselling skills at work, and formerly managed BAC. He has written *Death, Bereavement and Work* (CEPEC, 1992), and co-edited *Handbook of Counselling in Britain* (Routledge, 1989).

Danielle Douglas is a change consultant and counsellor and founding Partner of Phoenix Human Resources.

Ava Fine is an independent consultant and trainer to organizations. She was formerly Welfare Adviser at the English Welsh & Scottish Railway.

Tracy Goodman is a Senior Counsellor at Crewcare.

Guy Harrington is the Head of Counselling and the Trauma Unit at London Transport.

Jacki Harris is an independent consultant, specializing in management training and counselling, a BAC-accredited trainer, and former Chair of ACW.

Valerie Hopkins is Managing Director of Humanitas, combining her skills as a chartered accountant, investment analyst, trained counsellor and organizational consultant.

Michael Joseph draws on his many years of management and HR experience to work with organizations to effect and manage change, transition and personal development.

Ian Macwhinnie is a communications consultant and Shiatsu practitioner, and author of *The Radiant Kingdom: An allegorical study of meditation* (Celestial Arts, 1996).

Lynn Macwhinnie is a counsellor and training consultant specializing in holistic approaches to employee healthcare and career development, and currently Chair of ACW.

Jane Maitland is a management consultant working with businesses to communicate and implement EAPs.

Angela Mansi is a Senior Counsellor at Crewcare, British Airways.

Robert Nicodemus is an OU lecturer and internal consultant.

Andrew Rankin is Director of The Hanover Foundation, a charitable organization offering personal coaching for the 16-24 age group. He was previously Head of Professional Services for Methven Career Development Ltd.

Susan Scott-Parker is Chief Executive of the Employers Forum on Disability.

Maryjo Scrivani of Partners in Learning specializes in working with organizations to help people become aware of their possibilities when they are stretched to their full potential.

Margaret Smith is a counsellor, psychotherapist, trainer and supervisor, working as Staff Support Manager for the NHS North Mersey Community Trust.

Paul Smith is Head of Welfare and Counselling Services for Kent Police.

Carole Spiers has her own training and counselling consultancy, and is an occupational stress counsellor.

Peter Steddon PhD is a certified addictions specialist, with his own company, Mayflower Consultants.

Dr Beverley Steffert is a psychologist and author specializing in the physiology and psychology of communication.

Jenny Summerfield is Director of Summerfield Associates. She is a business psychologist and qualified counsellor. She is co-author of *Counselling in the Workplace* (IPD, 1995).

Wendy Tobitt heads her own consultancy specializing in communication management.

Mike Turner PhD is an executive mentor to organizations and a business consultant.

Carolyn Walker is a counsellor and trainer specializing in HIV/AIDS and psychosexual counselling.

Bridget Wright is a freelance consultant specializing in career issues within organizations and author of *Which Way Now: How to plan and develop a successful career* (Piatkus), now in its second edition.

I

A Context for Workplace Counselling

It is important for employers to find the type of counselling service which matches the needs of the organization. The articles in this section present some of the arguments as to what level of counselling input is required and how to distinguish between the various options. The section closes with examples of how some organizations have created their own unique employee support services, providing fresh insight into the concept of workplace counselling.

Is Counselling for the Organization or Employee?

Valerie Hopkins

When workplace counselling is directed only at the individual rather than the organization, it leaves many of the causative 'stressors' firmly in place.

*T*he sudden upsurge in interest in counselling at work in the UK has been brought about by a number of complex and interlinked factors. These include keeping up with modern trends, a movement away from the Thatcherite values of the 1980s, a need to give credence to other stakeholders rather than just shareholders and a wish to be seen to be benevolent. However, in my experience, the single reason companies seek help through counselling is to reduce excessive stress levels and their consequent harmful effects on both individuals and organizations alike. Companies want relief from pain, a direct parallel with the usual approach of an individual client to a counsellor.

Why such a growth in stress? Economic uncertainty both at home and abroad, a need to keep up with new, ever more competitive markets which undercut price structure, retrenchment and job losses due to restructuring, performance-related targets or new technology requiring new skills all mean that organizations and their employees have to deal with change to an unprecedented extent. It is this change (and the subsequent feelings of helplessness and lack of control) which leads to higher stress levels.

Addressing stress levels

Just as men and women may experience greater anxiety when losing the protection provided by their stereotyped roles, so can the 'post-industrial milieu' create greater anxiety by complicating and intensifying relationships across role and organizational boundaries. People work in an increasingly 'imploded' organizational environment.[1]

In a recent survey of 118 Chief Executive Officers and their wives,[2] it was found that nearly one in four are actively considering leaving boardroom life and that about the same number believe they are at substantial risk of job burnout. Yet workplace counselling programmes seem, in the main, to concentrate on the personal. Most appear to provide a valuable service in helping reduce anxiety in financial, marriage and family issues. These are, of course, fundamental to helping an employee both in terms of happiness, peace of mind and performance at work. However, stress at work is caused by a complicated combination of both personal and work-related issues and, in order to be really effective, counselling programmes at work must address both.

There is a temptation for companies to deny their responsibility as stress contributors by providing counselling programmes which project the problem on to the family. In this way, there is a risk that the employee becomes the patient or the one who needs treatment rather than the organization which can now feel benevolent and more in control. In Kleinian theory, a splitting has taken place. In reality, of course, the organizational stress has not been reduced at all. In fact, the danger is that the splitting may well have brought about an actual increase in stress levels as responsibility for it has now been firmly placed with the counselling provider outside the management hierarchy.

Therefore one must explore avenues in which organizations can be helped most effectively by the workplace counsellor. Clearly it is not our role to take on the mantle of the classic management consultant. Our role should be to help companies with the source of the stress rather than just the symptoms. There is a symbiotic relationship between employees, their employer and corporate health. Healthy employees lead to healthy employers and healthy profits, and the reverse is just as accurate.

Long-term programmes

Organizations, like individuals, will tend to look for the quick fix and easy answers and will look to us as counsellors to provide them. However, much as we can relieve the pain around presenting problems by providing counselling programmes, in the longer term we must find ways of helping address the issues at work. As in any good successful counselling contract, this will be achieved by building trust and confidence and helping the organization to find its own solutions. This may take some years. By researching, exploring and evaluating the organization's issues, cultures and climate before the commencement of the programme and then, within the bounds of confidentiality, by feeding back as much as possible on corporate problems, we empower the organization to help itself.

Mutual respect

This opens up a new role in counselling for organizational experts who have developed their clinical skills but it is essential for workplace counsellors to speak business language. They must gain the respect and trust of senior executives which will not be possible if they hide behind clinical jargon. There is also a tendency to look down on things we have not experienced. We have all heard clinicians belittle the commercial world and vice versa. If the clinical and commercial worlds are really going to help and work alongside one another then there must be mutual respect. This will only come about where there are trained experts who have experience of both.

Sometimes there will be no real wish or intention on the part of the organization to change. In this case, despite the possible loss of income, the only correct solution is for the provider to walk away. This takes courage. For any successful counselling contract, workplace counselling should be centred on empowering the organization to bring about change. We should not be providing 'sticking plasters' or 'laundry baskets'. We have a vitally important role to play in corporate health and culture in the 1990s and we should not underestimate our task. ●

Issue 5 Spring 1994

References:

1. Hirschorn, L, *The Workplace Within: Psychodynamics of Organizational Life,* MIT Press
2. 'The Stress of the Executive Life Style: Trends in the 1990s', *Employee Relations* Vol 13 No 4 1991.

Selecting a Counselling Provider

Jane Maitland

Research indicates that external counselling services are often used without a clear idea of what is available. The author suggests steps which may help in selecting a provider.

Counselling is coming off the couch and into the workplace, as organizations begin to look at the business case for helping their employees deal with the stresses that are an inevitable consequence of massive technological and organizational change. Evidence suggests, however, that external counselling services are often bought without a clear idea of the options available.[1] Every situation is different and, with the diversity of organizations seeking counselling matched only by the variety of providers coming into the marketplace, no hard and fast rules are possible. This article outlines a process to help HR (and other) managers select a provider. The list of questions may smack of the Spanish Inquisition, but the more you ask, the better equipped you will be, both to make the best choice and to build and support the case for counselling in your own workplace.

Analyse your needs

Time spent at the outset understanding what you and the organization want from the service will pay dividends. One of your first decisions is whether to provide in-house counselling or contract the service out. Although this decision can form part of your selection process, you may need to work with an external provider to sort through that first key decision.

Your main needs analysis should consider questions such as, what is driving the initiative (is it, for example, a directive from an American parent company, or feedback from an employee attitude survey highlighting increased levels of stress?). What do the different stakeholders, senior management, HR and line managers and employees, want from the services? Are those needs mutually compatible or exclusive? What support structures are already in place? Might it be possible to add on to existing resources, rather than provide a new service? What are the practical and financial constraints on the service?

Narrow the field

Put together a list of organizations specialising in the relevant field, such as the ones listed at the end of this article. Look for expertise that reflects issues relevant to your organization, such as substance abuse, ethnic minorities or redundancy. Ideally supplement your list by talking to people who have used counselling services in their organizations. Select the most likely looking candidates and contact around six or seven, briefly outlining your issues, and asking for details of their work. Most providers will supply you with some form of printed promotional material, though they may stress the importance of a meeting to explore your particular situation.

Draw up a list of three or four of the likeliest-looking. Arrange a meeting with each of the candidate organizations, and ask them to submit a proposal. (Most providers will not charge for this service, but you should confirm this in advance). Having the candidates present the proposal to you and your colleagues offers a good opportunity for you to explore their recommendations and begin the difficult process of deciding 'do we want to work with these people'. In the proposal and presentation, look for evidence that the provider has understood your problem, and has been able to add something to your own assessment of what is involved. Their experience is, after all, a major part of what you are purchasing.

What services are required?

Your needs analysis will have highlighted the key issues you want addressed, but think hard about precisely what services you require.[2] Do you want to provide face-to-face counselling or telephone contact only? If the former, how many sessions will you cover? If the latter, do you require 24-hour, 365-day-a-year cover, or will a limited hours service be sufficient? Do you wish to provide access for all employees and their dependents, or targeted employees only? Do you want the provider to help you launch the programme? If so, will they do site visits, or simply provide you with promotional material? What form of feedback will you require? Importantly, check for size. Is the organization big enough to meet your needs (do you have sites spread across the country?), or is it overweight for the service you need? Once you have agreed the services, make sure they are confirmed in a written contract.

Working together

Any relationship involving a supplier carries problems, and counselling services by their very nature touch on potentially sensitive issues which organizations may wish to ignore. The greater your confidence in the professionalism of the provider, and the stronger the culture match between your two organizations, the more you will be able to build and maintain a business case for counselling within your organization. This question of culture match, sometimes called 'organizational fit', is often the hardest element of the equation to define; it may also be the most important.

Some basic pointers are: has the provider taken time to understand your organization? Does the provider have a function (such as an account management function) which is designed to look at the organizational perspective and provide a link between individual counsellors and the management of your organization? Does there seem to be synergy between the values of your organization and those of the provider? Exploring questions around the importance of confidentiality, and the nature of the feedback and evaluation mechanisms you want to put in place, can help answer these questions. Perhaps most important of all, ask yourself, 'do you want to work with these people over a long period of time?' Listen to your instincts and discuss your personal response with your colleagues. You may find it valuable to visit the organization and talk to the counsellors, particularly if most of your contact to date has been with members of a management team.

Look for credentials

It is important that counsellors used by the service have undergone counselling training, hold credible qualifications, and abide by the codes of ethics of their professional organizations, such as the British Association for Counselling (BAC). Are the counsellors used by the service receiving supervision? from whom and how often? If the provider offers financial counselling, or legal counselling, check that the counsellors have relevant qualifications. If there is a management team, find out what professional qualification and credentials they possess. If it is appropriate, do they have professional qualifications in the field of Clinical Psychology (such as association with the British Psychological Society) or other clinical qualifications in the area of mental health and drugs and alcohol dependence? Is the organization a member of a professional body such as BAC and the Association for Counselling at Work or the Employee Assistance Professionals Association?

Draw up a contract

Once you have agreed the basic proposal with the provider, ask for a letter confirming details and costs. Make sure that the letter gives you a clear breakdown of costs. For example, how many consultancy days (if any) are included in the price? Is this charged on a daily rate. If so, what is the rate? What promotional materials (if any) are included? Are supplier fees costed out, or will they be extra? What training will be provided? What is the cost of the Helpline (if appropriate) and the face-to-face counselling? Are these charged separately or on an 'as-used' basis?

If you have not already done so, check that the provider is financially secure and be clear as to what insurance arrangements—such as malpractice and general liability arrangements—are in place. The letter confirming the proposal will form your legal contract with the provider; if there are any elements which differ from your understanding, or on which you require clarification, request clarification in writing. It is also worth stressing that any changes to the specification be notified—and costed—in advance, to help ensure that any confusion is avoided as the relationship develops.

Issue 12 Spring 1996

Reference:

1. Highley, JC, and Cooper, CL, *An Assessment of UK EAPs and Workplace Counselling Programmes,* UMIST, 1996.
2. *Counselling Skills and Counselling at Work: An introduction for purchasers and providers,* ACW, 1996.

Resources:

ACW membership network.
BAC *Counselling and Psychotherapy Resources Directory.*
Summerfield, J *Counselling in the Workplace,* IPD 1996 (contains a section on needs analysis).
The Personnel Manager's Handbook, IPD
EAPA publishes a Directory of EAP providers.

Adding Value to Counselling

Michael Joseph

Counsellors can provide valuable feedback to the employing organization, without being in conflict with their own ethical codes concerning client confidentiality.

W hen I am asked by a manager in an organization: 'Will you see Peter X for us, things are a bit difficult for him at the moment', the ensuing conversation is always attempting to seek answers to a series of questions. These are perhaps best summed up as: 'What exactly is the situation here?' and 'What am I being asked to do and is it feasible?'.

The fact that I am being asked at all gives some insight into the organization: it already believes that workplace counselling is worthwhile and is prepared to invest money in that belief. There are an increasing number of companies providing counselling of different kinds to employees, via such areas as personnel, health and welfare, internal or external counsellors and EAPs. What is less clear is the understanding of these organizations about what they can reasonably expect from the services they commission and what additional benefit might be obtained from listening to and using appropriate feedback, particularly from counsellors outside the company.

Facing vulnerability

We have seen widespread 'downsizing' over the past few years, with many organizations providing outplacement counselling as part of redundancy packages. How much 'real' counselling is done within these services is often a function of the style of the provider, but for many people there is a clear need, especially at the point where people feel vulnerable following a major redundancy announcement. The range of emotions associated with loss and separation are rife and unless these emotions are acknowledged and discharged appropriately, the energy and motivation for jobsearch or lifestyle transition are greatly diminished. This need is exacerbated where the values of the company have, for many years, incorporated a 'jobs for life' philosophy, either implicitly or explicitly, and where restructuring has necessitated a very public change of approach—just two examples from many being IBM and BNFL. These and other companies in both the public and private sector have responded to the commercial imperative to slim down the organization by offering 'voluntary' redundancy schemes, often with generous financial packages as an incentive. However, the message has been very clear that if the necessary levels of voluntary redundancy are not achieved, then the option of compulsory redundancy is likely to follow. In consequence, it is little surprise to find that not only do many of those leaving experience high levels of stress but also those staying, the so-called 'survivors', are often significantly affected and demotivated. How far can short-term counselling go to relieve the symptoms of these two groups or address the underlying issues?

There is much current focus on the issue of the survivors of redundancy, with increasing recognition of the existence of 'survivor syndrome' and the need to address this as part of the restructuring and remotivation process. Some companies faced with this situation, for example British Gas, have taken the opportunity to introduce EAP counselling support as well as outplacement support, thus providing confidential counselling for those remaining as well as those in transition. Counselling itself cannot change the work environment, but the counsellor will quickly become aware of any lack of congruence between stated or implied company 'vision and values' and what actually happens in the workplace. It requires great care not to collude with the client against the company, or individuals within it, though the counsellor will pick up a great deal of information which could be of considerable value to the company.

Perceived benefits

Increasing acknowledgement of the value of workplace counselling has made it easier to debate counselling provision with companies, though there are still many who either consider it an option only for the weak, or are unconvinced of the bottom-line financial benefits. Among the companies which do perceive a benefit, managers' attitudes can vary widely, even within the same organization. Many are very supportive but even they can often have misplaced notions about the function and purpose of such services. 'Patch them up and get them back to the front line' is still commonplace as is the concept of transferred conscience: 'We know things are unreasonably tough here, that's why we are providing these services, to show the staff we care'.

Great care needs to be taken by those offering workplace counselling services to set realistic expectations of what outcomes may be possible and to gain clear agreement to the 'counselling contract' being established. Absolute confidentiality is an ethical 'must' which most of my client companies readily accept, though they are sometimes tempted to ask questions like 'I know you can't give me details, but how is old Peter? Do you think I can rely on him doing a good job for us or would it be advisable for me to be thinking about a successor?'. Refusing to be drawn on such issues while maintaining the relationship with the fee provider requires the exercise of good counselling skills!

What feedback can be given and how can a company make best use of it? As a counsellor with a management background in large commercial organizations, my experience is that I never undertake counselling sessions without gleaning information that is of potential value to the company and which can almost always be disclosed without breaching confidentiality. Where I provide counselling on a regular basis or, say, as part of a large-scale exercise, then the perception and bias of a single client are cross-checked with others. Although the primary focus of the sessions is the client's personal material, what emerges is a clear overall view of what the staff feel it is like to be within the organization and what are the major sources of dissatisfaction. I can usually form a view not only of the overall management style but also of the perception of different managers' individual styles. Where a company is prepared to seek or listen to the views of an 'outsider', this information can provide invaluable feedback, in effect additional management consultancy.

In summary, undertaking a workplace counselling assignment requires a clear understanding of the requirements and expectations of the client, mutually resetting these where necessary. Both parties need to be clear that the counsellor cannot make good organizational deficiencies or personal limitations of its managers and supervisors. From those many counsellors who have good experience of the workplace environment themselves, a client company can obtain considerable feedback of high quality and value if they are prepared to ask for it. This can only be truly beneficial if they have a mechanism and willingness to use it positively. Counsellors, for their part, will need to give the feedback in a constructive manner, bearing in mind the history, background and current issues being faced. All parties can thus gain additional value from what is already a beneficial service.

Issue 8 Spring 1995

Balancing Integration and Independence

Catherine Carroll

The author sees the future as one where 'multi-skilling', for all employees not only counsellors, is the norm. Her research indicates the large number of roles which all workers must play.

L iterature on the subject of workplace counselling is almost exclusively in favour of integration, believing it is the only way to influence the wider organization for the benefit of employees. Independence and integration are the essential yet paradoxical qualities of workplace counselling. This is turn must be a reflection of the counsellor's own integrity and professionalism as a 'bridge builder', forging contacts between the worlds of counselling and business.

This is no easy task for the workplace counsellor, needing to find new ways to address unexpected tensions and conflicts ethically. Workplace counselling services are still in their infancy, and this presents developmental issues but, while some say counselling and business cannot sit together, this is not my experience. It again, however, raises the question of whether workplace counselling requires its own code of ethics, which takes into account the needs of the organization as well as those of the client.

Implicit in this idea of integration is 'multi-skilling' i.e. how can counsellors be counsellors as well as perform a range of other roles. More established services have found this a natural development as well as a reflection of the workplace itself. This is seen in the USA, and my UK research in 1993 demonstrated 12 additional tasks such as training, welfare, health education, facilitating organizational change, advising managers, etc. In turn, this exciting diversity requires counsellors to be acutely conscious of boundary issues and confidentiality. Traditional counselling has been purist in having one role with clients. In reality, workplace counsellors are almost certain to have various roles bringing them into contact with staff. This can be an encouragement when the counsellor is seen to be approachable, professional and have integrity.

One particular area where integrated services can make a contribution is in managing the human side of transition. Counsellors are skilled in managing change and all our work is around being with others experiencing various forms of life change and therefore have something to offer our organizations in helping staff at those times. Yet this is also a tightrope, how to advise on any issue effectively and not become over-engaged with the politics and territorialism that accompany organizational transition. This could be seen as 'siding with the enemy' by some staff and, as such, violating independence. This has implications for confidentiality. It is important that workplace counsellors be public when they can. There can be too much mystery around counselling, and confidentiality may slip into looking like secrecy, and that is not helpful.

Diverse roles

Having diverse roles in an integrated service helps demonstrate effectiveness and value—a word of caution, however. The deep commitment and enthusiasm of workplace counsellors to move into these wider tasks can shift into over-commitment with the risk of burn-out. It is not usually worrying about clients that keeps counsellors awake at night—it is the organizational politics! This is tricky because wanting to make a difference for the better is seductive; it is difficult to let the moment pass, not out of laziness or lack of will but as a measure of self-care and good modelling.

While I suggest that, ideally, workplace counselling be integrated and independent there may be a place and/or a time for such services to be seen to be, not isolated, but 'apart'. Initially, it may be necessary to signal to staff the separateness of the service by its physical isolation. Once confidence in its independence is established then moving to a more integrated position becomes possible. We also need to recognize the developmental stages of the organization and the counselling service. I found that the key to accepting my frustration with the organization was to respond to it as a client, respectful of resistance, pace and stage of development as well as acknowledging its strengths and resources.

The individual clients, however, remain the prime focus of workplace counselling; they must remain central to the work of internal and external services. They give it meaning and purpose. The measure of our effectiveness and understanding of the individual clients is the measure of our personal authority to speak to the organization about other issues.

In conclusion, keep what is best from the past, adapt it to the present and anticipate the needs of the future. There is then the natural move from a position of separateness to one of integration where the role of the counsellor is seen more clearly to be of relevance to the wider needs of the organization. This is the experience of those services that have been in place for some years and, having earned respect, are invited to contribute more fully to the life and well-being of the organization. This is an exciting and challenging responsibility which requires balancing professional independence and integration. ●
Issue 18 Autumn 1997

Ethical Considerations

Jenny Summerfield

*The author makes a plea that any counselling skills training
should be introduced within an ethical framework. A checklist of
questions reduces the chances of later regret.*

*T*he Human Resources Director was feeling particularly pleased with himself. He had wanted some counselling skills training for his team and the training provider had assured him that all the people attending their short course would be 'professionally accredited' at the end of it. 'Real value for money', he thought, 'and I won't need to give them any further training.' This is essentially a true story relayed to me by a client company during a recent meeting. Of course, some details have been altered to preserve confidentiality. Like many human resource professionals, this director only wanted the best for his people. He was also not equipped to pick his way through the minefield of information about accreditation and he, quite naturally, believed the 'expert' supplier.

All properly qualified counsellors will know the road to professional accreditation is a long and arduous one. And so it should be. Naturally, the claim being made by the training provider in this story is false and we must hope that such extreme breaches of ethics are rare. However, it cannot be denied that many training deliverers are jumping on the bandwagon of the fast growing workplace arena and, if we surveyed them, I wonder how many of them would be adhering to the BAC ethical guidelines?

There is also the important consideration that not all providers will be members of the BAC or other professional bodies concerned with the ethics of counselling. As there is no possibility of regulating such people we need to consider carefully how we can improve the situation. One suggestion would be to 'educate' the buyers. To this end, human resource professionals might find it useful to ask any or all of the following questions of skills training suppliers:

➢ *'How much do you understand about the workplace context?'*

Delivering counselling in the workplace is unlike developing personal counselling outside of work in many respects. Role and boundary conflicts come into place. For example, line managers will find it difficult to be counsellors to their own people because they often hold the power of promotion or salary increase. Talking about difficulties to their manager may hold the fear for people that it is an 'admission of failure'. Perhaps the line manager should be trained only to recognize where someone is in difficulty and to refer internally (to HR) or externally. Human resource teams can have more success in that they are separate from the line, and issues of trust and confidentiality are less problematic. They should therefore receive a more sophisticated level of training. Their role conflicts are more about switching roles between staff appraiser, coach and counsellor, and skills trainers will need to have an understanding of the organizational systems and processes that HR people need to work with.

➤ *'What qualifications and experience do the trainers have?'*

Are they counselling psychologists or holders of a recognized qualification? Training a group in counselling skills can be little different from directly counselling. The group are emotionally vulnerable, and so are the clients that they work with. Because counselling is a subject that is concerned with human emotions, group members may well find that certain subject areas tap into their own experiences. They can be surprised by an unexpected rush of emotions and may themselves need some counselling from the tutor. We should perhaps consider whether it is right for trainers who have no counselling training or experience themselves to train others. How will they recognize and handle such group vulnerability? This brings us on to the next question.

➤ *'Does the trainer understand the referral process and will they be able to communicate it clearly to the group?'*

Essential as a safety net for clients seeking help is that those acting temporarily in the role of counsellor understand their own limitations in comparison with a full time counsellor. Properly trained counselling professionals will know that 'failure' is success in counselling situations, i.e. to say that a client's issues are beyond your skills and refer them to a specialist or more experienced counsellor is a sign of a mature and well-balanced person. This situation is the exact opposite to what happens in people's work roles where such an admission would be seen as a real failure. A good trainer will help the group to accept and work within their own limitations.

➤ *'Is the trainer a practitioner undertaking ongoing supervision and personal development?'*

Non-counsellors may not have the depth of experience and may not seek supervision. Supervision by a specialist or more experienced counsellor is a professional must. We all have our limitations, we are all continually learning, and we all need support. Trainers should build in some form of follow-up case-work meeting after a training event or at least suggest that such supervision should take place on a regular basis for those who will counsel others regularly. Aside from this, trainee groups should be encouraged to meet regularly for mutual support. Supervision will provide a safety net for clients and will develop the skills of the group further. It will be helpful, once again, if the supervisor has some understanding of the workplace context.

➤ *'Does this person have the right "lightness of touch" when work-ing with the self-awareness aspects of the training?'*

Some people have suffered gratuitous 'self-development' exercises on programmes where they have been left with unresolved and painful issues to sort out on their own. As mentioned earlier, sometimes people are 'surprised by their emotions'. This is quite different from the kind of experimenting with 'group dynamics' that some trainers indulge in. A personal example: as a counselling skills trainer, I have to look after the 'walking wounded' who have been on such courses, been given unwanted and unsupported feedback, had no counselling follow-up, and been left to 'stew', sometimes becoming quite depressed. A good counselling skills trainer will know how to work with any appropriate and spontaneous 'group process' issues without 'forcing' the group to open up their inner thoughts and feelings. Quite simply, it is not what they have 'signed up for' in attending the course, unlike potential counsellors who know what they are letting themselves in for when they embark on professional training. Where the trainer is not a counsellor, do they perhaps need a counsellor on hand as a support tutor to handle any personal issues that may arise?

These are just some of the issues that could be called 'good practice' in skills training. Hopefully, human resource professionals will be able to draw on such information to help them formulate the right questions to ask of a potential supplier. Unlike other kinds of skills training, counselling can impact either favourably or disastrously on people's lives. Perhaps we, as professionals, should be asking if we can do more about potentially dangerous practices from suppliers.

A final, if obvious, recommendation would be that all buyers of counselling skills training should be familiar with the BAC Codes of Ethics and Practice and the IPD Guidelines. A personal wish is that all of us who have a vested interest in seeing ethical practices in training, work together to make things safe for organizations, safe for the people finding themselves temporarily in the role of counsellor and above all, safe for their clients.

Issue 8 Spring 1995

References:

BAC Code of Ethics and Practice for Trainers.

Nelson-Jones, R, *Practical Counselling and Helping Skills* (3rd edition), Cassell Educational Ltd.

Philips, K, & Fraser, A, *The Management of Interpersonal Skills Training*, Gower Publishing.

Counselling Skills at Work?

Jacki Harris

*As counselling seeks a more professional image, it is important to
be clear about the different levels of competence and skills training
required to meet workplace needs appropriately.*

*I*n the workplace there is still confusion and misunderstanding about the distinction between counsellors and counselling, and the use of counselling skills, even though many organizations have introduced counselling services for their employees using EAPs or in-house counsellors. Perhaps it is more a question of terminology and the time has come for us to think about the words we use to describe the activity. BAC defines a counsellor as: *'someone who deliberately and voluntarily contracts with a client (individual, couple or group) to provide counselling'*. The aim of counselling is to: *'provide the opportunity for the client to work towards living in a more satisfying and resourceful way'*. Definitions for counselling skills seem to hinge on the set of skills or tools that the individual uses, and do not clearly identify the boundary with counselling. It seems to be a very grey area.

Differentiating between skills

By differentiating between counselling i.e. what the counsellor does, and counselling skills as everything else, we miss out the important activity that is often undertaken by managers and HR professionals trained in counselling skills. These managers are not counselling, and in using the term counselling skills it does not capture the essence of what they are actually doing. While they may be using a counselling approach and utilizing specific attitudes and skills, they are going through a problem solving process. This is very different again from the manager who employs the use of interpersonal skills to 'listen' to an employee.

Consider the following scenario: Susan has been knocked off her bicycle and is lying injured in the road. A bystander who has recently completed basic first aid training goes over to help. It is evident that Susan is badly hurt and all the first-aider can do is attempt to stem the bleeding and keep her as still as possible until the paramedic arrives. The paramedic assesses her injuries, administers drugs for the pain and secures her on the ambulance for the journey to the hospital. On arrival the doctor decides Susan needs emergency surgery and so she is transferred to the surgeon. Each of these individuals were aware of their levels of competence, based on training and experience. We would not expect the first aider to perform emergency surgery. This is, however, what can happen to managers who have attended a short course in counselling skills and return to their organizations and thereafter are known as 'counsellors'. The expectation from the organization is that the manager can 'counsel' anyone, with little or no support. This is of course unrealistic and is likely to fail. Often the manager's own expectation is that if they are unable to deal with the employee's problem, thereby necessitating a referral, it implies they have somehow failed.

Using the medical model as an analogy, we all have an understanding of the different roles and the limits of competence for each role. We could use a similar continuum for counselling (as in Figure 1). As you gain additional training and experience, you move towards the role of the counsellor with recognized qualifications and professional membership.

If we reassess the simple distinction between counselling and the use of counselling skills, we can differentiate between three different roles:

1. *Those who incorporate counselling skills into their work role* These are interpersonal skills and include active listening with empathy, responding, reflecting, acknowledging feelings, attending to verbal and non-verbal clues. They are used by line managers, supervisors and trainers in everyday interactions with colleagues, staff and customers where they are utilizing specific skills to facilitate communication. They are used in a variety of contexts, often where the agenda is set by the manager, e.g. appraisal, coaching, mentoring, exit interviews.

2. *Those who are problem solving using a counselling approach* The manager is demonstrating the core conditions of a counselling approach: acceptance, genuineness and empathy in order to develop a relationship with the individual he is seeking to help. Some of the key factors which differentiate this activity from 'using counselling skills' are:

- it is a specific relationship with a clearly defined contract for problem solving; it has boundaries; is time-limited; and confidential within the organizational constraints
- it uses a model for the process with a theoretical basis and is not just a range of skills
- the manager works within a code of ethics and practice, e.g. BAC.

Where managers undertake such an activity it is important they receive adequate training and also appropriate support. The training would be delivered by someone with experience of counselling skills training and counselling, e.g. BAC-accredited training. The supervision or consultancy support would help to identify process issues and where personal issues impinged on the manager/'client' relationship. A training organization which has added counselling skills to their portfolio and expects trainers with no counselling background to deliver the course is far from ideal.

3. *Counsellor* This category would include those who are professionally qualified having undertaken a significant period of training. The counsellor may work in-house; as an EAP or on an *ad hoc* basis for the organization. It is essential they have experience of the context, are familiar with organizational systems and structures and also understand the complex issues around boundaries, confidentiality and role conflict.

To see how this might work, let us consider the following: Jim has been arriving late for work, seems to be short-tempered with his co-workers and on a couple of occasions been rude to customers. Alan, his supervisor, has recently been on a counselling skills course (one-day basic) and so uses his new skills to 'actively listen' to Jim who says he has domestic problems but is reluctant to say any more than that. Alan refers Jim to the line manager (who has attended a 6-day intensive counselling skills training for managers) who uses a counselling approach for problem solving. The manager identifies that Jim's wife has left him and the children, leaving him to cope with everything including the dropping off and collecting the children from school. The line manager and Jim decide on an action plan whereby Jim is able to deal with the domestic difficulties by rearranging shifts and having more flexible work hours, whilst he sorts out more permanent child care arrangements. Jim is very upset and angry about what has happened but the manager does not feel equipped or experienced to deal with this, so refers Jim to the EAP counselling service or suggests he could see a Relate counsellor.

In this scenario, each person has worked within their limits of competence and training. One way forward in the debate would be to acknowledge problem-solving using a counselling approach as a specific activity valid in its own right. Then we can avoid the confusion of trying to categorize everything under the catch-all title of counselling skills.

Issue 19 Winter 1997

An Intervention Assessment Model For Managers

Paul Smith

*Knowing when to refer can be a challenging issue for managers,
especially those who have training in counselling skills. This
article introduces the idea of a useful assessment framework.*

*I*n my own experience of counselling at work, managers continually ask me at what stage they should refer on to the counsellor. As a check for them, I request each to ask a question of themselves: 'Do I have the time, expertise and resources to deal with this problem?' If the answer is negative to all three elements, then referral should be considered. As a rule of thumb, this works well on certain day-to-day issues. It is easy to identify that as a manager you may not have skills in bereavement or relationship counselling and referral to an in-house or external counselling service is what is required.

Unfortunately, life is inevitably more complicated than this and this complexity is reflected in the problems which managers and supervisors encounter when dealing with employee issues. Running an in-house counselling service has meant that I am faced with the prospect of training specific groups of people on how and when to refer. In order to do this, it was necessary to develop a model of intervention and referral which reflected common sense and did not denigrate the abilities of the manager. It was also necessary to re-emphasize that the duty of care for the employee still rested with managers and that we as counsellors were an organizational function which existed to advise and support them in that role. It is not in the manager's or employee's interests to refer every issue to the counselling service.

The model

Developing an intervention model was made relatively simple through my contact with Stewart Greer from the Kent Council on Addiction. He has developed a model of assessment for alcoholics based on Prochaska and DiClemente's Cycle of Change, and I have adapted his model for my own use. I believe that many of the strategies used in the addiction field can be successfully transferred to general workplace counselling. Because such counselling is inevitably brief intervention, accurate assessment and focused strategies assume a greater relevance in dealing with the client.

The background to the use of the model revolves around the concept that employees presenting with a problem either possess or do not possess the skills and motivation to do something about that problem. The employee is in the process of trying to cope with a situation which is stressful or crisis-laden. He or she is trying to achieve a balance between the demands of life and their ability to cope, or there is a need to change the nature of the situation or their reaction to it in some way. Management intervention in employee problems must take into account the motivation to change, and the level of skill the employee has to make that change or manage the crisis. Misjudgement in this area will result in a failure to address the problem correctly and may lead to further intensification of the stress or crisis.

SKILLS	MOTIVATION: Willing	MOTIVATION: Unwilling
Competent	PROVIDE: ● Support ● Reassurance ● Facilitation of change	● Generate alternatives (do you want to change?) ● Provide information ● Motivational interviewing
Incompetent	PROVIDE: ● Life skills training, eg goal planning, assertiveness, time management	PROVIDE: ● Information ● Minimal intervention

The matrix

The assessment of motivation and skills is made on the basis of a scale for both areas. In terms of skills, the question to ask is: 'Are they competent or incompetent to make the changes needed?' and, in terms of motivation: 'Are they willing or unwilling to make those changes?' The answers to these questions will help the manager to decide on an appropriate intervention, provide a common referral language, and avoid being sucked into time-consuming use of 'counselling skills' which may prove inadequate. The matrix created by this process is shown in the illustration. Each quadrant has discrete interventions which will help the manager to feel comfortable with the course of action to take when assessment has been made.

Willing/Competent—In terms of an employee presenting with a problem, this is the most gratifying area. It is also the area in which managers can be most successful. The major intervention is providing support. Active listening, reassurance and maybe facilitation of the situation (time off for appointments, etc.) will help the employee feel valued.

Willing/Incompetent—While many people are willing to deal with problems, they may lack the skills to do so. If the skill is readily identifiable and available in-house or through local training, then this may be a good first option. Identifying distinct skills may not be possible so referral from this quadrant is quite common.

Unwilling/Competent—For those who are assessed as unwilling, the major task is to examine the ambivalence of the person to change or to manage the problem. Motivation, the 'state of readiness or eagerness to change',[2] is the central issue. One of the more recent developments in the addiction field is that of motivational interviewing, which is a series of techniques which can be used to help the client explore problem behaviour and to move towards change. This process is helpful in this quadrant. Generating alternatives and giving information in relation to the problem area can also be useful but care is needed to avoid creating resistance by establishing 'either/or' scenarios. Referrals to counselling are common.

Unwilling/Incompetent—Here motivation and skills are both deficient and the phantom of the 'reluctant client' comes to mind. Minimal intervention is common with provision of information and feedback, in the hope that the person receiving it may move from a stage of not being aware that change may be needed to one more conducive to positive intervention.

Working with managers and referral agents within an organization, I have found that the matrix gives ready access to understanding the initial processes of assessment and need to refer. Allowing for the fact that any theory or model is a map for understanding reality and should not be confused with reality itself, I feel that sensible use of this idea will help in clarifying referral problems, generate understanding of employee involvement in providing their own solutions and empower managers to use their 'counselling skills' without feeling they are getting in over their heads.

Issue 3 Winter 1993

References:

1. Greer, S, and Roberts, N, 'Motivational Interviewing' *Aquarius Study Packs,* Birmingham, 1992.
2. Miller, WR, and Rollnick, S, *Motivational Interviewing: Preparing people to change addictive behaviour,* Guildford, New York, 1991.
3. Smith, P, Roberton, S, and Kennett, R, *Interventions: Victims by profession,* Kent County Constabulary, 1993.

Peer Counselling Provision

Tracy Goodman and Angela Mansi

The authors give an insight into a unique, internal counselling service tailor-made to the needs and requirements of British Airways cabin crew.

February 4, 1985 saw the birth of an innovative service provided for the cabin crew within British Airways (BA). The idea was originally launched by three BA cabin crew members, concerned about the stresses and difficulties that the flying lifestyle can sometimes bring. These crew members approached the airline for their support of the initiative. As a result, the Crewcare counselling unit was born with 14 cabin crew selected, recruited and trained by Professor Gerard Egan to provide crisis counselling for the cabin crew community.

Crewcare is totally independent of any other department within BA, with a service unique among airlines. It demonstrates that people who are in the business of providing a high degree of service and care for others, need and appreciate those qualities being available to themselves from time to time.

Comprehensive training

Today the Crewcare team consists of 18 male and female cabin crew counsellors, including two senior counsellors who provide ongoing professional supervision and training for the group. The team are drawn from the Heathrow and Gatwick community, with at least three years cabin crew flying experience on the long and short-haul sections of this working area. All counsellors are recruited through a careful selection procedure, and undergo a comprehensive training course, based on the Egan Problem Solving Model. Ongoing training and supervision, both inside and outside of BA, takes place on a regular basis, keeping the counsellors abreast of new developments, social issues and changes affecting the cabin crew community within the airline. The confidential service provides a worldwide 24-hour telephone coverage (freephone in the UK; overseas calls to the direct-dial number can be reclaimed) as well as face-to-face counselling during office hours, 365 days a year without appointment.

The 'drop-in' counselling service, to discuss any issues which may be of concern, whether work-related or personal, is situated in the BA Compass Centre at Heathrow Airport. As the main operations centre for all cabin and flight crew personnel it makes the unit very accessible. There is also the facility of ongoing counselling from either of the senior counsellors within the group. The unit can also help with any further information about support agencies or helplines, etc.

There has been a slowly won but successful acceptance from the flying community that the counselling service offered is completely confidential and run by cabin crew for cabin crew. This has been achieved by continuing to maintain strict boundaries and ensuring the integrity of the service by adhering to the BAC Code of Ethics for Counsellors. The unit operates totally independently of the rest of the airline and this position is respected and understood by British Airways. Since the inception of Crewcare 12 years ago, BA has recognized the value of this peer group counselling service and continued to fund its operation. Indeed, the department's presence, directly in the workplace, is a measure of the support and credibility of Crewcare today. It is now one of the most established facilities available to crew from their first day of flying.

Support systems

As well as the confidential helpline, Crewcare also runs a seminar for women shortly going on maternity leave and another seminar titled 'Return to Work' to help with the transition back into the workplace. Recently incorporated under the Crewcare counselling group umbrella is 'Working Parents', another support facility to help crew meet the diverse challenges which can be posed in combining the rigours of a cabin crew lifestyle with that of parenthood. While this service is currently used predominately by women, we are hoping to encourage the attendance of the men who are also new to fatherhood. There is also a Network Support Group which puts members in touch with other cabin crew in their area to exchange ideas, give and receive general encouragement and a chance to discuss childcare options. The rapidly changing nature of the industry in staff scheduling and services can bring its own particular problems and fears for those crew who are returning to work after absenteeism from long-term sickness (anything over six weeks). Crewcare offers voluntary monthly workshops to ease a person back into their job and provide some reassurance and support in addressing their anxieties.

The cabin crew community, by nature, is a very self-supporting group and individuals often take time out to listen to each other's concerns and problems. However, the Crewcare counselling unit emphasizes the immediate availability of a trained counsellor who has a true sense of the lifestyle that goes hand-in-hand with being a member of the British Airways flying community. ●
Issue 16 Spring 1997

Listening Ear Network

Ava Fine

The development of a resource of staff trained in counselling skills has become an integral part of employee support at the English Welsh & Scottish Railway.

Employee Assistance Programme (EAP) versus in-house counselling is one of the traditional debates within any organization considering the costs and effectiveness of employee support schemes. The volunteer approach is paying dividends for the American-owned English Welsh & Scottish Railway (EWS), formerly the freight side of British Rail. Following privatization and reorganization, we tried to develop as comprehensive a counselling service as possible. In my role as the only in-house counsellor and with limited resources, it was obvious that I could not meet all the counselling requirements of a nationwide company with a workforce of about 6,000 people. The railway culture was also steeped in its own tradition, custom and practice, and counselling was not a process readily accepted or understood by either management or employees. Many people did not feel at ease in coming forward with their problems to anyone who was not seen as part of the company culture.

Volunteer counsellors

Before the amalgamation, there were small networks of volunteer counsellors, who originally were trained to be listeners in harassment and equal opportunity matters. We decided to combine and extend these groups. All applicants had to go through a rigorous selection and assessment process which consisted of an interview, group discussion and a role play. Successful individuals then embarked on a comprehensive four-day counselling skills course, on which they were also assessed. This was a two-way process and, if applicants were not happy with what was expected of them, there was the option to withdraw. We now have 30 volunteers covering an area from Motherwell to Penzance and Bristol to Peterborough. They come from every area of railway life: drivers, shunters, clerical officers, shop floor workers, supervisors and administrators. Staff have the backing of their managers who often allow them time and a room to use when seeing those seeking help. In the main, the volunteers see individuals from either their own or a nearby location though in theory they could speak to anyone in the company.

All the counsellor contact numbers for the service are advertised monthly in the in-house newspaper, with regular special news features. Each volunteer has an added responsibility to 'spread the word' in their home depots. They do this by speaking to local management and trade union representatives and by displaying contact numbers on notice boards. A colleague and myself supervise their practice and we have regular network meetings which always include a training session, an information slot and supervision.

The volunteers are well aware they are not 'professional counsellors', and the referral process—either internal or external—is part of their practice. As for their motivation (they are not paid) in developing new skills, all of them say how much they have gained personally, not only in helping others but in also getting to know themselves better. Does the organization consider it a success? The service is certainly not without its problems. A few counsellors who have not had as many clients as others have suffered from a lack of commitment during the period of organizational change. Some managers are not as supportive as others and, on occasions, it is not always easy to contact the counsellors. In the main, however, it has been a success, opening up a counselling provision to employees who may not have considered using it before and providing an added resource in times of uncertainty. Confidentiality has been of concern, but now that the service has been in existence for some time, employees increasingly trust the volunteers.

Additional training

The company is now viewing the network as an integral part of its employee support programme. There is a possibility that the volunteer will receive additional training in critical incident debriefing to enable them to conduct such work in the event of an incident or accident. Their remit will be quite specific and only those volunteers who are willing to take on this extra role will be trained. In the event of a major incident they could be asked to provide additional support to the professionals. The fact that many of these volunteers are operational staff themselves would be an added bonus in these circumstances.

For myself as supervisor and counsellor, it has been a challenging but effective exercise, with the volunteers handling over 60 contacts and enquiries each quarter. The service has certainly demonstrated to employees that we care and there are people with the right skills on site to talk to if a listening ear is needed.

Issue 19 Winter 1997

Supervising
Workplace Counsellors

_____

Michael Carroll

*There are many potentially difficult and challenging situations
that can arise for the workplace counsellor, and supervision is an
important tool for clarifying the counsellor's boundaries.*

here are several areas of particular interest to the supervisor who is working
with counsellors in organizational settings—what follows are two of them.[1]

*1. Helping the counsellor live and work within the organization, and to
be clear about the roles and boundaries that are part of their work.* Counsellors
in organizations are employed by the organization, not by the client, and are
both employees of the organization and counsellors to other employees within
the Company. These roles demand clear thinking so that responsibilities to the
organization are clear, as are the responsibilities to the individual clients. How
these are viewed and decided by the counsellor may not be shared by the
organization. There are many ethical dilemmas. Where does the counsellor's
primary responsibility lie should there be situations where the good of the
organization and the welfare of the client seem to be in conflict (i.e., where the
counsellor is party to information shared by the client that is detrimental to the
Company)? What sort of independence does the counsellor have in making a
decision about referral without consent of the Company?

Though authors may sometimes claim that these are clear-cut, in reality
it does not always work out simply. There is little agreement in the literature
about where primary loyalties lie. Some are absolutely certain that the
counsellor's major responsibility is to their clients, and others equally certain
that the primary responsibility is to the organization (after all, it pays the
salaries). Ethical Codes do not give answers to many individual situations, and
it is here that supervision can provide the forum that alerts to ethical sensitivity
and allows for reflection preceding decisions. What is clear is that counsellors in
organizational settings do more than engage in individual work with clients.
They have a concern for the welfare of the organization, and in some sense
'counsel the organization' as well as the client. Otherwise they can get caught

in the contradiction of helping empower individuals to make decisions about their well-being and watching them be adversely influenced by a system that may be destructive of that well-being.

The supervisor is constantly monitoring the professional issue of relationships with the employee counsellor. A key question to the counsellor is: what relationship do you have with this person? Are you the trainer, the consultant, the advisor, the publicist, the counsellor, the advocate, or the work colleague? Where relationships are not clear then all sorts of interpersonal games are played out. Especially difficult are areas where the relationship changes. A participant on a stress training course suggests coming for counselling, a counselling client wants an advocate in her forthcoming divorce case, a work-colleague hints that she wishes to talk about her personal problems, a client wants to form a closer interpersonal relationship, a manager who is being helped with personal problems asks for help with departmental relationships. Is it advisable to move from one set of relationship roles to another with this client? What are the implications? Would referral be better?

Since those who provide counselling from within organizational settings engage in a variety of roles and relationships, then assessment of client needs becomes a key issue. Helping counsellors set up methods of initial and on-going assessment is crucial for clarifying intervention strategies, and helping maintain the clarity of the helping relationship. Assessment can also be made from an organizational perspective. In other words, is the client coming because of poor management within their division? Not all problems are intrapsychic: some are situational, some interpersonal, and not a few systemic.

Control of information

2 Supervision is the forum that helps the employee counsellor control the flow of information within their domain. Redundancy counselling is an area particularly open to 'loose' information which often creates double-binds for counsellors. The company-client often reveals information to the counsellor about the individual-client that the counsellor is unable to use. It may be about their personal life (e.g., he had a breakdown two years ago and saw a psychiatrist for six months; we have had a number of complaints about her way of dealing with subordinates) or about their professional life (e.g., she is a loner and unable to work within a team).

What does the counsellor do with this information? In other circumstances the counsellor would feel free to share this with the client as a basis for their work together. From a company perspective it may not be possible to do so. The counsellor is caught with a 'secret': on one hand she or he has inside information about the client, on the other hand she or he cannot share it. And what happens when/if the client discovers that the counsellor knew and never disclosed that they knew?

Dealing with the flow of information, what information is required, what happens to information given from sources other than the individual client becomes a key focus at times in supervision. Part of the supervision strategy is to help the counsellor control who knows what about whom, and direct how and what they want to know. Well intentioned managers can burden counsellors with information they would be better not knowing. Part of the supervision is enabling the supervisee to educate the organization to information flow.

On the other hand, it is the task of the counsellor to feed back information into the organizational system. Of what use to an organization is a counselling provision if it cannot listen to information from it and adapt its policies accordingly. Besides dealing with referring managers and work-supervisors, counsellors are in a prime position to make recommendations about life within the organization, about management styles, about team work and interpersonal relationships, and about the key problems faced by employees. This can be done in formal and informal ways: annual reports and statistics, training courses in counselling for managers. Supervision has a key role to play here and much valuable time can be spent on rehearsing methods of informing the company about issues that might help it change.

Issue 10 Autumn 1995

This article is the author's abstract from his book, *Counselling Supervision: Theory, skills and practice* (Cassell, 1995).

II

Change Management

The impact on everyone in organizational upheaval is particularly acute when those involved are caught unawares, or when good practice has not been implemented. Communication and careful preparation was key to BNFL's experience of change, and the NHS North Mersey Community Trust implemented a multi-faceted approach to supporting stressed staff. These two articles highlight successful outcomes while other authors raise questions on the inappropriate use of counselling services through uninformed management practice. The perspective of the individual employee and of the counsellor comes into sharper focus with a glimpse at useful techniques and tools which can be used in managing careers in a climate of change.

Is Counselling being Used to Paper over the Cracks?

Valerie Hopkins

Organizational change puts pressure on all those in the company.
Consultants and counsellors need to question and evaluate their
own role in facilitating the change process.

The rise of media announcements of business re-organization programmes seems to be consistent and inexorable; with counselling playing a valuable role in any successful change management programme. This is as it should be; as experts in how people change, counsellors are well placed to help in moving employees forward. My concerns, though, are not based on the utilization of counselling per se but rather in the way it is being used in organizational change, the motivation for its introduction by management and the political climate into which it is being introduced. These factors all have a profound effect on whether any reorganization can be viewed as a success, both from a macro business view and the micro perspective of an individual employee.

Pressure to downsize

At the beginning of the 1990s, managers' perceptions of the effect of the global market and the economic situation drew them to the concept of business process re-engineering; if organizations were to survive they would have to reformulate the way in which they functioned. At the same time, as the power and possibilities of information technology began to appear endless so the use and value of people seemed less important. Unfortunately, this headlong rush into re-engineering helped to eclipse the alternative approach to organizational design—that of the Tavistock's socio-technical school—which had offered a prescription of change since the 1940s. This approach incorporated a concern for people rather than axing jobs, and a design approach that increased both efficiency and the quality of working life.[1]

The movement toward re-engineering also had a reinforcing effect on the attitudes and beliefs of senior management to their roles and responsibilities in the process. Never an easy relationship, it seemed that the new model provided justification and substance to the rationale that employees, were, in the main, a cost rather than a valuable resource. Despite excellent profits, many organizations started making people redundant as a way of being seen to be applying best human resource practice. This policy was supported by evidence of the pressure on large corporations, by shareholders, to downsize.[2] Furthermore, business school education continued to hold as one of its central tenets the view that services should be out-sourced as much as possible as a way of reducing 'people' overheads; at the same time, there seemed to be an apparent rush into a follow-my-leader policy.[3]

As management became less sure of their sense of direction so it seemed that the only way forward was to follow competitors with swingeing reorganizations or to stay one step ahead by mega-takeovers where dual functions were streamlined. The first serious doubts about re-engineering surfaced in 1994 when the 'McKinsey Quarterly', based on projects in more than 100 companies, concluded that re-engineering had often been simultaneously a great success and a great failure. Dramatic results in individual processes were accompanied by a decline in overall results. From then on problems increased, many pioneering companies found that they were left with processes that were more difficult to manage than the old structure, with increased costs and alienated and demoralized workforces. In November 1994, the *Economist* asked Michael Hammer, the architect of re-engineering, what had gone wrong. He replied that many firms had equated re-engineering only with downsizing and other 'slash and burn' exercises in cost reduction. He said 're-engineering is about rethinking work, not eliminating jobs'. At the same time, a survey found that only 16 percent of senior executives were fully satisfied with their re-engineering programmes, whereas 68 percent were experiencing problems.[4]

Conflicting messages

The trouble was that the fear and uncertainty of the change process itself had resulted in a radical splitting of perceptions, attitudes and behaviours of leaders. While mission statements asserted the increasing value of employees, behind the scenes there was brutalization of the workforce; while most employees were encouraged to make themselves as flexible and mobile as possible, a few were so valued and needed that their salaries and profit shares became the size of lottery prizes; while some employees were told there was no work at all, the rest were often told directly or indirectly that the price of working was a job with no flexibility either in time or duties. You put up, shut up or got out; there were plenty of people out there ready and willing to take your job.

Re-engineering programmes as often as not, were introduced in the language of 'beginnings'. Words such as 'project' and 'new starts', 'implementation' and 'strategy', 'optimism' and 'success', used at a time when employees were staggering from the shock and uncertainty of job losses, reinforced their belief that management were out of touch with their feelings and did not really care anyway. Loyalty and commitment, the very stuff on which goodwill is built, went out of the window almost overnight. Little time was given for transition to allow people to come to terms with the changes before the next round was introduced. The external consultants employed to design the re-engineering process took pride in their role as business strategists. There seemed to be little recognition of the people costs involved.

Owning responsibility

It is therefore inevitable that the success of re-engineering as it is currently perceived is being questioned; it is linked to fear, oppression and loss. Employees do not see it as a great opportunity but rather as a way to keep shareholders happy in the short term and at their expense. Yet organizations and their staff must constantly evolve if they are to survive. Both must accept the natural uncertainty of transition if they are to develop. It is the current organizational denial of responsibility that brought about so much damage and has resulted in so few change management programmes being seen as successful. Stress management, career counselling, EAPs—they all ultimately place the problem, and therefore the responsibility, with the individual. Fine as it goes; we are all responsible for our own stress levels and careers, but what about the effect of the quality of the relationship with our employer? How many organizations are owning their part in all this? How many are introducing systemic changes in organizational relationships to meet these challenges? In my experience, there are very few indeed. Bion emphasized how difficult it is for human beings to relate to each other in a realistic way in a joint task.[5] This is perfectly illustrated in the saga of re-engineering. Responsibility for the pain has been fragmented onto 'them', for example the shareholders, the emerging market competitors and global competition. Fear and anger have been projected onto the employees. Effective resolution is only possible when an organization can address the heart of the matter and make relevant changes there.

The counsellor's role

As counsellors, I would therefore invite you to think carefully about the role you are fulfilling in any change programme. Are you yet another golden key to open up the possibilities of maximization of return? Are you an instrument of denial of the pain caused by current organizational life? Are you a way to demonstrate to employees that they must take responsibility while allowing organizations to deny their own? Change management programmes can and do work. However, it takes courage and understanding at a very senior organizational level to bring this about. It takes a commitment to group values based on ethics, real integrity, compassion and trust. It takes a willingness of leaders to deal with their own vulnerability and pain as well as that of others. It takes skilled training and education in interpersonal skills so that most of the 'caring', when relevant, can be carried out by managers at work rather than being siphoned off to an external agency. It takes imagination and courage to empower employees, to delegate rather than abdicate,to lead by guiding rather than by controlling.

Working partnerships

In any change management programme, external consultants and counsellors should see their role as working in partnership with the client organization, but also with the ultimate aim of doing themselves out of a job. As in one-to-one counselling, the objective should be to become part of the system for a limited time and then withdraw once the pattern of communication in the organization is functioning healthily and relevantly to the circumstances of the situation. The risk is that we get to see ourselves as indispensable. This denies the empathic potential of leaders and their responsibility to care for their organizational community. Successful leadership is a difficult job of balancing imperatives, of caring and discipline, of retaining and letting go, of giving and taking. I believe our role is to support and educate organizations as they gradually learn this. It is this role in the change process which is all important, not the product.

Issue 13 Summer 1996

References:

1. Trist, EL, & Bamforth, KW, 'Some social and psychological consequences of the longwall method of coal-getting', *Human Relations* 4, 1951, pp.3-38.
2. Worrell, DL, Davidson, WH, & Sharma, VM, 'Layoff Announcements and Stockholder Wealth', *Academy of Management Journal* Vol 34, 1991, pp.662-678.
3. McKinley, W, Sanchez, CM, & Schick, AG, 'Organizational downsizing: Constraining, cloning and learning', *Academy of Management Journal.*
4. Munford, E, & Hendricks, R, 'Business process re-engineering RIP', *People Management,* Vol 2 No.9, May 1996, pp.22-29.
5. Menzies Lyth, I, *The Dynamics of the Social,* Free Association Books, 1989, pp.26-44.

The Human Challenge of Change at BNFL

Gregg Butler

At the 1996 ACW annual conference, the author gave an account of the challenge of restructuring at BNFL, and the role of counselling in implementing the company's new structure.

*L*ike many organizations, British Nuclear Fuels (BNFL) faced major changes at the start of the nineties, when competitive pressures forced it to undertake radical restructuring. Unlike other organizations, the company could not afford to have a bad shift and re-run the production line to get the product right. Between 1980 and the mid-nineties, the nuclear industry went through a sea change. From a cost-plus system (where we charged what it cost to reprocess fuel and then added on 15 percent profit) in the eighties, where the key challenge was to keep BNFL's name off the front pages, we moved to a position in the early nineties where the pressure to change became overwhelming. Industry overcapacity, price pressure from customers, and the Nuclear Review—alongside internal pressure and support needed for new business development—meant that BNFL had to find new, more efficient ways of working.

Strategic direction

The company grasped the need for change, and devised a radical restructuring, aimed at making the organization more focused on the strategic direction of the business. The change was driven by the top team, who worked together closely to devise the new structure and the Group Values that underpin it. A structure consisting of a vast Magnox Division with some small businesses and functions clustered around it had developed organically over many years. After gaining real commitment from the top management team involved (with much late night anguish and risk of liver damage!), we used a process we devised ourselves to divide the whole operation up into individual operational units—bricks—and put these together to form blocks, using criteria such as customer, regulator and other stakeholder views. Once we had gained consensus around a particular structure, we sent the provisional heads of the businesses away to produce bottom-up plans to see if the overall savings were worth the effort and risk involved. They came back with plans that would save £100 million a year.

Risk factor

To be successful, the restructuring had to be management-driven, and that meant that line management would need training. This involved coaching/counselling skills training; stress management workshops and education; training in how to give 'good' and 'bad' news. From the start, we were aware that there was a real, human, cost to the restructuring. Up to 1,500 employees would lose their jobs over the five years from 1994 to 1999. We knew that the change would cause pain to others, but knew also that we had to accept that this would happen, be caring but implacable. We had to go forward, consistently, with the changes. Yet the risks were significant; we knew that, if the situation was not handled properly, the possibility of suicide was real. Even if there was 99.9 percent certainty that people would not be overstressed there could still be seven individuals at risk out of 7,000 involved. All the posts in the group were considered and people were either given a post in the structure or in a project role. Then 3,000 people were told that 500 of them did not have jobs in the main structure.

Channels of communication

Communication was central; we knew that we had only one chance to get it right. Letters were sent to employees at their home addresses. Then provisional new directors and direct reportees briefed all the employees on the next layer of the structure. We must have been doing something right. There have been no claims of constructive dismissal and so no industrial tribunals.

It is not in the Cumbrian persona to seek outside help, but counselling was a central plank of the strategy. Counselling was available via an independent confidential helpline, from the line managers and from the HR/welfare/medical services. However, over the three months of the helpline only two people contacted it. Some 100 have contacted the independent counselling services, 300 the line managers and 100 the HR/welfare/medical route.

Job counselling was offered to all, to assist those who wished to seek new employment outside BNFL. For instance, one man took an HGV driver's course to change his area of expertise. The company had been using a firm called Doctus in the 1990s. At Sellafield they were used to raise awareness of the fact that Sellafield was ESTJ (Myers Briggs' Extroversion, Sensing, Thinking, Judgement) almost to a person. One of the Doctus personnel was employed by BNFL to head up the Human Resources Department at Sellafield, and this person's exposure to outside business experience was an essential part of the jigsaw in Fast Forward.

The new structure has been successfully implemented on time: savings and production targets met or exceeded in the first year, senior manager numbers reduced by 30 percent, significant reduction in management layers, values increasingly adopted, employee support maintained and business understanding increased. As always, it is not all plain sailing; conventional safety performance remains well below benchmark industries; 'vision assumptions' have not been implemented quickly or as fully as intended and progress in out-sourcing is slower than hoped. Some issues remain to be tackled: information and management systems remain inadequate, re-engineering of key business process has only just started and a self-sustaining momentum for change is not yet established. That said, there is much to be proud of: savings targets are being met, safety and morale did not slump and continuous improvement now takes over. The change did cause anxiety and anguish but all reductions were voluntary and we did not have any serious incidents.

Learning from change

So what did we learn? That far reaching change with stretching targets can be achieved, but the boundaries of empowerment need to be clear. Long-term management focus on priority areas is vital, individual commitment to personal change is necessary. In particular, all the members of a team need to know their strengths and weaknesses, and to realize that, in some areas, the team might be relying on one of their weaker areas. Commitment to grow the roles needed for a particular team is essential. The concerns and influences of stakeholders should not be underestimated, especially in a company like BNFL which relies heavily on the support of its local communities and has a big responsibility to them.

Importantly, fairness and decency have a major part to play. The communications did succeed in explaining why we had to restructure and there was a widespread recognition of the business rationale. The fact that people were being dealt with humanely and fairly appeared to decrease the level of reaction to people who were included in the structure. A lot more human management training would, however, have made the ground more fertile for the change. If I had one piece of counselling-related advice to give to anyone contemplating a similar initiative, it would be that once everyone understands *why* things are being done, there is at least a valid backdrop against which personal discomfort and loss can be rationalized. If the *why* is not clear, even this comfort is denied.
Issue 14 Autumn 1996

Surviving Downsizing

Bridget Wright

Conflicting issues often arise for those left behind after a downsizing programme. The need to rebuild teams and confidence is often overlooked, especially in the wake of budget cutbacks.

Recently I was talking to a director of a large multi-national. He recounted his experiences of masterminding a reorganization within his company and his remarks echoed with deep and bitter memories. The experience had been very stressful and, prior to the fateful announcement, he had demonstrated quite serious stress symptoms. Reflecting on the events of six months earlier, he was able to point to many positive outcomes. The downsizing part of the operation had been handled by an outplacement company and statistics showed a high percentage of the redundant employees had found new positions, often with improved prospects. His present concern was the difficulty in achieving his new objective: of rebuilding his team for the exciting future. He was facing a mixture of resistance, distrust, fear, anger, demotivation, disinterest, low productivity, hostility and overall lack of interest in the new tomorrow, and he could not understand it. None of his ideas during the last six months had led to any change. In fact, he felt the situation may have become worse and he could not understand why his team was so negative: 'they should be jumping for joy, they have a job.' Here lies the key to the problem—a popular misconception that those who remain after downsizing are the lucky ones. For many it is the opposite. What they see is former colleagues in new jobs, often with better salary packages and a nice lump sum in the bank. They have the chance to explore new opportunities, new routines, learn new skills, even taking the plunge into self-employment and, sometimes, realizing the dream of a lifetime. I don't want to paint an entirely rosy picture. Redundancy does bring many serious problems, but good news travels faster than bad. Successful individuals want to advertise their achievements to their former colleagues.

Initially, the individual who still has a job often feels guilty ('Why was I saved?'). Guilt can often turn to anger when the reality of the situation is assessed. The company has lost a number of people and workloads will stay the same. In fact, workloads dramatically increase, often without clear communications or rational forward planning. The new organization plunges into chaos.

People realize that nobody is responsible for certain jobs and arbitrarily these become the responsibility of those who remain. Gradually employees acquire new jobs which they do not want (nobody communicated any rationale), cannot do (nobody provided any training), have no time to do (nobody assessed their workload), and have no interest in (nobody asked for their view).

The anger is fuelled when the company is seen to spend large sums of money on the departing individuals. From the perspective of the employees left behind, they face nothing but cutbacks. No resources for the extra workload they have to perform, no salary increases, bonus or Christmas party, etc. All they perceive is more effort for fewer rewards and senior managers communicating the message that they should be grateful. Anger is quickly replaced by fear. 'What if I am next? When will the next wave of job cuts hit the department?' The fear results in demotivation, disinterest, decreased output, and if allowed to spread, the overall result is organizational ill-health. Many businesses are displaying these symptoms at present, which is also indicated in various surveys and research studies.

Professor Cary Cooper from UMIST states that one in four main board directors are actively looking to change their job. Government figures relating to depression show a major increase and the underlying cause is increasingly attributed to greater pressures at work. These symptoms will not disappear. They need treatment, if organizations are going to meet the challenge of the future growth and development. Unfortunately there is no simple remedy, but the best starting point is to confront the issue. If you have recently been involved in any major change initiatives which have resulted in redundancies, reflect on how the survivors have been treated, and what the organization has done to harness the commitment of these employees.

Issue 3 Winter 1993

Interventions during Organizational Change

Margaret Smith

Counsellors need to recognize that individual and organizational stress are closely interlinked. Often, the individual can only benefit to the extent that organizational stressors are addressed.

*T*ackling the issue of stress amongst staff at a time of rapid change became part of my brief as Staff Support Manager for the NHS North Mersey Community Trust (NMCT), a 'second wave' Trust formed in 1992 composed of three previously separate units. As one of the largest community and mental health Trusts in the country, it employs about 3,000 staff, half of whom are nurses. In the first three years of its existence, and as part of the requirement to achieve a viable financial position, two hospitals were closed and there was a reduction in the workforce of 21 percent. In the summer of 1993, at the height of the restructuring exercise, the Staff Support Service was set up. This was supported by the results of a 1992 research project which indicated that a clear majority of the staff felt they would benefit from the provision of a Staff Counselling Service. Initially this was to provide counselling, staff support groups, supervision and stress management training for staff. I have subsequently extended this to include critical incident debriefing (Trauma and Crisis Support). One of my priorities was to address the levels of stress experienced by staff having to cope with so much change.

Recognized links

Anyone providing staff support should be mindful of the link between individual and organizational stress. It is suggested by Hinchelwood[1] that in any community there will be a complex relationship between the individual and the group in which an individual is selected to express the mood of the group because they have 'some specific adaptability or valency for a role needed by the community'. The word valency is a term borrowed from chemistry and means the way in which atoms combine together to form a tight bond. He explains that, by this, he means there is a 'happy fit' between the internal world of the person selected and a particular aspect of the current life within the group, which they need to dramatize. An example of this would be that a bereaved staff member in a hospital which is under threat of closure might be vulnerable to being unconsciously assigned the role within the organization of expressing something for the whole team.

Stokes[2] talks about the institutions that people work in as being containers—receptacles for their psychological and emotional anxiety. He says that people are able to use their workplace to project parts of themselves that they do not want to be aware of, into other, more distant parts of the organization. These comments are often global ones such as, 'Managers don't care about us, they are only interested in balancing the books'. In order for this process to be maintained, however, it requires the organization to remain relatively stable. Stokes suggests that when conditions do not provide such an environment, it is likely that there would be 'an increase in interpersonal tension and personal stress within sub-groups inside organizations, instead of the more familiar and simpler tensions between workers and management'.

Addressing stress levels

The National Association of Staff Support suggests that there are three levels at which it is possible to intervene in relation to stress at work: the individual, the group, and the organizational. One of my first objectives was to set up a staff counselling service and to work with the training and development department to increase availability of stress management training by developing a team of specialist trainers. The staff counselling and stress management courses are aimed at the individual level, and are the most widely available form of support. As a provision on its own, however, there is a danger that it can be seen to imply that all problems are due to individuals not coping, and that once these people are put right, all will be well. It has been written elsewhere the importance of treating the cause and not the symptom; the individual is often the symptom. To avoid this the Trust has given priority to intervening at each of the three levels.

Staff consultation groups are aimed at the group level. This is a less used, but I think an effective form of intervention and I have been involved in two types of consultation group: the first being where a staff group have requested ongoing support because they are working with a demanding client group, such as the terminally ill. This type of group is effective in helping staff express feelings. The other type was where the request was made as a result of a crisis. This may be, for example, where staff are not coping well with a very challenging client, or because workplace changes have led to increased tension within the staff team. This second type of group normally involves only a brief systemic intervention, which focuses on the way in which one part of the organization relates to another.

The facilitator needs to clarify any request for this form of help before agreeing to work with the group, as it could be that what the staff group want is really something else, perhaps clinical supervision, or the need for more managerial support. Nevertheless, this exercise can be valuable in itself for the staff group. As with individual counselling, it is important that the group facilitator ensures, as far as possible, that the issues which the team present are really issues that the group can deal with, and not the result of an unresolved problem somewhere else in the organization. In my experience, this is often a significant factor in the request for help.

Organizational ownership

Organizational interventions, usually calling on external consultants, can be one way of tackling the stresses inherent in the culture and management systems of an organization. Stapley[3] talks about organizations having their own distinctive personality and suggests that the creativity of staff can be enhanced by good management which provides support and containment of anxiety, particularly at times of change.

The Chief Executive of NMCT and the management board decided to participate in the organizational initiative developed by OPUS for the Health Education Authority. The aim of the intervention was to reduce high stress levels and to increase staff creativity. Of significance in selecting this particular intervention was its focus on the organization taking ownership of the process including the diagnosis of the problem and the development of its own solutions. The CEO appointed a Stress Management Group consisting of Trust staff to oversee the project. The diagnostic event involved a representative sample of staff focusing for two days on the things which caused them stress in their jobs. This was a demanding task and at the end, a daunting list of stressors, such as communication problems and tensions around change, had emerged.

The consultants then facilitated a two-day workshop to help a group, mainly of managers and including the management board, to develop strategies for reducing these stressors. This has included reviewing communication procedures and setting up a committee to develop a policy for the management of change. Since then, the stress management group has met regularly to facilitate the implementation of the strategies that emerged from the workshop. This has proved to be a worthwhile but challenging task and it will be some time before it has been completed.

There is no clear line marking the border between individual and organizational stress—one is intertwined with the other. It is important for the counsellor or group facilitator to be aware of the link between the two and to ensure that any intervention is addressed at the appropriate level or levels. Ideally, an organization will be involved in reducing unwanted stress at each level. This will help to ensure that the provision of services such as staff counselling, stress management interventions and staff consultation groups do not focus their interventions only on the individual or group, but also give attention to organizational stressors at times when the root of the problem belongs there.'

Issue 18 Autumn 1997

References

1. Hinchelwood, RD, *What Happens in Groups: Psychoanalysis, the individual and the community,* Free Association Books, 1987.

2. Stapley, *The Personality of the Organization: A psychodynamic explanation of culture and change,* Free Association Books, 1996.

3. Stokes, J, *The Unconscious at Work in Groups and Teams: Contributions from the work of Wilfred Bion,* 1994.

From Employment to Lifetime Employability

Mike Bagshaw

Adapting to the end of the 'jobs for life' notion is a necessity for most. We need to widen the range of our useful skills and take responsibility for handling our careers.

We are living in the age of micro-technology. Computers can do so much that it sometimes feels as though people are obsolete. Jobs, promotion prospects, career possibilities, business large and small—they all used to seem eternal. Now they are disappearing like dreams. There is only one thing we can do in the face of such change—we can change ourselves.

In the old world, firms were sometimes described as 'like a big family'. The employers were like parents, taking care of employees like children, who in exchange worked hard and behaved themselves. It worked on a carrot and stick principle—the carrot being security, perks and a pension, the stick being the threat of losing these things. That particular carrot is extinct. The stick looms large, whether employers wish it or not, because there is no such thing as job security. There is nobody able to tell employees what they should do. The new way forward is for everyone to participate, to keep alert, to try to see round the next corner, to adapt and learn new skills, and to be ever prepared to adapt again.

It is a sad fact of life that people resist change, largely because it scares them. Many of today's managers had it drummed into them at school that they only needed to work hard to find wealth, comfort and security. Now, in midlife, they realize it is no longer the case. Many react by 'playing safe', continuing to work hard in the ways they know so well, but it just is not safe any more. Far from protecting their jobs, they are decreasing their employability by stagnating in the same old skills. This sets up a spiral of stagnation, both for the company and the individual.

Individuals trying to protect themselves do not take risks. That means new ideas are not tried. So the company does not grow, does not generate wealth and is not in a position to offer good rewards. This makes people even more worried about their future, so they cling harder to the old ways in the hope that their job will be safe. They gain no new skills to offer elsewhere, so have low employability. They are actually less safe, but the stick of threatened unemployment keeps them in their place.

Attitude shift

Nothing removes that stick, but having an array of skills does much to bring it under control. The boost of confidence puts individuals and companies on a growth spiral. Individuals, freed from fear for themselves, work towards the future of the company, thus generating growth and wealth. The company can then offer good rewards, individuals are carried forward by their increasing self-development, which gives them more employability, and so it goes on. It does not come easily. It requires a major attitude shift. It means letting go of the comfort of entitlement and security, grasping instead self-responsibility and self-development. The skills required cannot be defined far in advance, as though there were an appropriate box of knowledge for any given career.

One of the many necessary skills is the ability to 'think outside the box'. It means learning in different areas such as the technical and financial, as well as the so-called 'softer' skills, like team working, relationship building and focusing on customer service. People who are merely adequate will not succeed in a competitive world. They must look to enhancing the future both of their company and themselves, contributing all they can rather than simply playing an assigned role. Even good performance no longer guarantees employment, but it does improve employability, which has to replace job security as a personal goal. The change should not be one-sided. The whole contract needs to be renegotiated. It is no longer an adult-child relationship where the employer takes care of the employee who serves the employer in return. Instead, the two sides collaborate with a mutual commitment to the creation of wealth and/or value. This goes hand in hand with the personal development of the employee. Companies with this ethos can create high morale even when permanent employment cannot be guaranteed.

Continuous transition

Employees need to be in a continuous state of transition preparedness so they can move quickly to new employment. They have to take charge of their own careers: they need to manage their own finances, keep a healthy life style and keep their CVs up to date. Nobody will see to these matters for them. This necessitates some strategic thinking. Immediate concerns and the competencies required today may be at odds with the long term needs for career progress and future employability. Time needs to be set aside to consider the importance of each. People need to reassess their core purpose. What do they really want? This needs a good deal of personal strength, much of which comes from family strength, so they neglect their home lives at their peril. They need strength too for the continuous striving—to keep abreast of new developments; to be visible in the business world; to maintain strategic networks; and to grasp any opportunities that come their way. Counselling has a key role to play in helping people to find personal fulfilment and meaning in the new realities of the workplace. Helping people to help themselves, to regain a sense of control and personal empowerment is the essence of counselling.

It is also fundamental to lifetime employability in contrast to the parent-child relationships in the traditional paternalistic work culture. These concepts go to the heart of values and beliefs conditioned from the early years. It is not surprising therefore that the change to more adult-adult psychological contracts between employer and employee can be uncomfortable for some and even painful for others. We know from research that the quality of one's support system is a major factor which mitigates the adverse effects of stress and change. In particular, it is support which challenges people to be their best and to be proactive which is most helpful. Overprotective caretaking, which does things for people which they could easily do for themselves, ultimately makes people feel like victims. Provided people have access to good quality support, the change to an employability culture can be a positive trigger for real empowerment, personal growth and job satisfaction. ●

Issue 13 Summer 1996

Redundancy and Change

Carole Spiers

Two different sides of change are: redundancy for those required to leave, and adaptation to the new order for those who stay. Counselling has an important role in both.

Redundancy forces change on an organization and the people within it, both those staying and those leaving. The reaction of both these groups can be influenced by the organization and a positive outcome will result in beneficial consequences for the individual as well as the organization. Changes in an organization will often reflect on such issues as job status, job content, relationships with peers and supervisors, working conditions, and numerous other aspects of a person's job. The whole organization tends to be affected by change. Even when managers use their most logical arguments in support of change, employees are frequently unconvinced of the need for it. It is not so much the nature of the change as the employee's attitude towards the change which is crucial. Consequently, to try to help people come to terms with change on the basis of logical argument is ineffective because the logic will not have a direct effect on feelings. The effective use of counselling skills can help but they need to be used alongside practical organizational initiatives.

Resistance to change

People will generally resist change. Despite this there is often a counter-balancing desire for new experiences and other associated gains. Change can, in whatever form it takes, be successfully managed. If it is not, however, then problems will emerge in the form of lower morale, poor communications and a decline in confidence in the organization and its management. Management initiate most changes and therefore the responsibility for achieving change effectively lies with them. It is the employees however who will influence the final outcome since it is they who actually implement the changes. Employee support is therefore essential: in redundancy this means those who are staying. Communication with and involvement of employees is essential and a special effort is needed to stabilise social processes in times of change. While some will welcome change as an opportunity to achieve new goals, others may react differently. There may be fear of job loss and associated income and/or status, as well as altered relationships with people. Where change requires the person to work different hours, travel to different sites, move to a different position within the offices or workshop or even relocate, then the impact begins to affect social activities. Relocation of employees involves uprooting both the employee and his/her family.

Loss of a job through redundancy can mean that a significant part of the person's identity is lost too. Self-confidence is eroded and the person can feel excluded from society. Familiar work routines are comforting. Despite 'being in a rut', few would actually consider changing that rut for something new and unknown. The fear of that unknown is basic to all resistance to change. Change and uncertainty go together and both contribute feelings of discomfort, which redundancy heightens. For some, re-employment may seem remote and unlikely, the loss of structure and activity difficult to adjust to. Anticipation of the consequences of change in an organization is frequently worse than the change itself. Rumour, conjecture and secondhand knowledge of changes elsewhere all combine to generate fear of change and subsequent resistance to it.

Counselling for employees

The effects of redundancy can fall anywhere on a continuum from total disaster causing a maximum crisis level with resulting trauma and shock at one end of the scale, to a time which will give pleasure and excitement at the prospect of leaving the company with benefits, at the other end of the scale. The company should provide resources and counselling support to minimize the negative effects of redundancy on staff and their dependants together with support to deal with the subsequent effects of redundancy on those employees remaining who will have to bear the brunt of additional duties of productivity.

Redundant employees may undergo a severe crisis or simply raised stress. Counsellors or personnel staff need to be able to gauge the individual's state of mind and to respond appropriately. Crisis situations are totally new, unpredictable, psychologically paralysing and they pose a shock to the emotional system. They catch the victim unprepared. The absence of a repertoire of responses that have worked in the past is most disturbing because people spend much of their daily lives operating on 'automatic pilot' relying on tried and tested behaviours. An individual's response to crisis depends on his or her philosophy of life and the strength to survive. The background history of coping with other crises will also be important and in addition to this the individual's attitudes, both positive and negative, to change.

Counselling management

The surviving manager has to find out as much accurate information about the company's position that is available and must establish what can and cannot be told to employees, having regard to commercial confidentiality. The manager should know who is going and who is staying in the department and be the one to personally deliver 'the bad news'. Management will need specific crisis intervention counselling skills training for this difficult task and cannot be expected to deal with it effectively if they are not given the appropriate support, preparation and training from the organization, while at the same time refraining from taking on the role of counsellor in its deeper professional sense. This role is best carried out by the personnel department or employee counsellor. The manager should be supported in his turn by a central counselling resource able to deal in depth with those employees who are manifestly more deeply disturbed or depressed by the situation. This resource should be available not only to those made redundant but also to those who are staying, including managers who feel unable to face the situation and those affected by it. It may also be possible to set up a facility whereby small groups of redundant employees may meet to discuss mutual problems and to exchange ideas.

The future

The future may look bleak for those whose jobs are going, and feelings of anger, bitterness, fear, etc., will abound. It is vital that everything is done to ease the way ahead. Companies have a responsibility to be clear as to their resources at this time, both in relation to those ready to help as well as the moneys available. The goodwill generated will ease some of the pain, but also provide the company with a way to restore its image (always damaged by the redundancy situation), its identity and confidence in the community. This is essential for the future, for those who continue to work there and for those who may return to work there if things improve. Those who are staying with the company may have many varied and mixed feelings—relief that they have not lost, but guilt about those who have, and worries about security and prospects for the future. If the company does as much as it can for those who are leaving, it will help the morale of employees who remain. They know that the company they work for will do its best to look after them, in spite of what has happened. If the company does little or nothing, motivation will be affected for a long time to come.

Issue 8 Spring 1995

Mapping and Managing your Career Path

Andrew Rankin

The author introduces the idea that we, as individuals, can take more control over our career path. Management of our career is also something that needs to be kept under regular review.

uch has been written and spoken about how change is affecting organizations and employment patterns and how, as individuals, we need to adapt in order to survive. Noted authorities on the subject provide us with dire warnings about the future; we read their books, nod sagely but continue as before. Why? Perhaps there is no single answer as to how we, as individuals, can manage our careers and, indeed, destinies.

But what does career management mean? The dictionary definition of 'career' is 'a progress through life', a path which we have the opportunity to identify and have more control over. Change in business practices, geopolitics and expectations has meant the destruction of the trust between employers and employee. In other words, it is down to us, as individuals, to identify and plan our 'progress through life'—because organizations can no longer guarantee any security or longevity in this relationship with us. So, what do we need to do in order to take the first steps in the management and mapping of our career path?

Four stages

There are four separate stages that we must explore in the dynamic process of career management ('dynamic' because the process is continual).

Stage 1—The personal stocktake

It seems obvious that if we are to take charge of mapping our career path, we should know what it is we have as our internal resources. We must address the question, 'What am I?' If we look at this first stage as being the foundation of our career path mapping, then there are a number of bricks that need identification. Some are common to us all:

Skill—What skills do we possess? If we need to review our portfolio of skills and determine what of our skills we are most comfortable using and which we prefer to use. However, most of us have forgotten what we can do, or just take our skills for granted.

Achievement—What have we done in our careers to date? Employers are now requiring performance rather than attendance and we must be able to demonstrate the former. Big questions are being asked by employers about our individual contributions to the business.

Strengths—These are our innate qualities. Unlike skills, we do not acquire strengths but we can develop or play them down as we like. Like our skills, we have some qualities with which we are more comfortable than others.

Weaknesses—As much as we all have strengths, we all have weaknesses. It is important to recognize and own these; we can then exercise choice as to whether or not we do anything about them. Some weaknesses can hinder our career development—we have the choice whether or not to take action.

Values & Needs—We all have values, those things in life which are important to us and which provide us with motivation. If we become aware of our needs then the identification of what will contribute to our satisfaction (and performance at work) becomes easier. All too often, we neglect our values and needs; they are subjugated to the needs of others around us including organizations and employers. This can lead to a feeling of unfulfilment or dissatisfaction.

Reality—In mapping our career path, we must keep our feet firmly in the realm of reality. Reality is individual and relates to issues such as home location, income requirements, partners' careers, children's education and other such facets of our life. Through this awareness, we construct a more realistic approach to the mapping process. Indeed, one question we must ask ourselves is 'How fixed are the constraints in my life' and what, if anything, can I practically do about them.

Energy—For energy read stress. Whilst we all need an element of stress in our lives to motivate us and give us energy, when the stress becomes unmanageable, problems relating largely to health can occur. Exploration of how stress effects us can assist in developing avoidance stategies.

Attitudes—By exploring our attitudes to change, to styles of working and to our relationships, for example, we can determine our preferred way of dealing with them. Change is dynamic in that it will never stop. We must identify the ways in which we deal with change and adapt or modify where appropriate.

By exploring these foundations, individuals will have a greater insight into themselves than before. This insight will enable them to plan for the future and, more importantly, cope effectively with the vicissitudes of life.

Stage 2—Exploring options

For many this stage is the most challenging because it involves an element of creative thinking. Because of our social conditioning, our left brain is dominant; the analytical, logical part of our brain. At school we learn things by rote; we are discouraged from asking 'why?' and there is a strong element of 'Do as I say and not as I do'. For this reason, the creative, intuitive part of our brain, the right brain, is underused and repressed. There are three blocks to creativity: high intelligence, arrogance and negative thinking. Heightened awareness of the importance of right brain thinking has spawned numerous ways of creative thinking, such as Brainstorming, Mind Mapping and NLP. Underlying all creative thinking activities is the requirement to be non-judgmental. All too often, when we think of a possibility we consign it to the dustbin with a 'Yes, but'. When we think creatively we should park our judgement until a more appropriate time.

Stage 3—Setting objectives
Every day we set objectives—for others, often for our employers. We need to become more comfortable in setting objectives for ourselves, objectives that relate to our careers. Very often, we miss the point about this because we identify objectives which are so 'far away' that the attempts to reach them are doomed to failure. The result? We give up trying and abrogate responsibility for mapping our careers. It makes sense therefore to set realistic objectives or steps to reach our goal—bearing in mind that changes in circumstance may affect the larger, long term goals. Therefore, our objectives are more of a series of stepping stones rather than one giant leap. In setting these objectives, we must be aware of what personal attributes we possess and how these can support us along our career paths.

Stage 4—Monitoring and maintenance
Career management is a dynamic process. Like any planning activity, the implementation requires monitoring and adjusting if necessary. How can we do this? There are many ways, such as:

The annual check-up—Many people have regular, usually annual healthchecks. They're given a '10,000 miles service' to face the rigours of the next 12 months. Why not do the same for careers? It may be in the form of investing in a relevant book (of which there are many); of attending talks or lectures or going to see a career counsellor. Most people spend more time and money on planning their annual holidays than their careers.

Mentoring—The concept of mentoring is gaining credence in this country. The mentoring relationship can be with a person who is either work or non work related and who provides advisory support to an individual on a regular basis.

Objectives—If we regularly check our objectives and how we are progressing them, we can monitor our progress. Circumstances change and if we are to cope with these changes, we must adapt as necessary.

Career management is important and, for many reasons, we can no longer trust others to manage our careers for us. The speed of change is increasing and in order to meet the challenges, successfully, in our own terms, a high degree of self-knowledge is needed. The four stages of career management are one way in which we can help ourselves to meet the challenge of change both in work and outside—a way to manage our own 'progress through life'. ●

Issue 11 Winter 1995

Executive Mentoring

Dr Mike Turner

This article identifies an important way in which career options can be kept under review. There are many additional benefits, both personal and professional, to be gained from mentoring.

Organizations increasingly need to be able to reinvent themselves to stay aligned with, and responsive to, their customers and other stakeholders. Creating the necessary changes can involve a wide range of programmes and initiatives such as culture change, process re-engineering, benchmarking, total quality management, values alignment, and so forth. What all these have in common is that, to be successful, they have to be accompanied by behavioural change by the organization's stakeholders and, in particular, by the organization's senior executives. Executive mentoring is an intervention designed to support such senior executives and other key staff in making the necessary behaviour changes.

The term 'mentoring' covers a range of categories of intervention and types of working relationship. The form of mentoring described in this article has as its goal that of increasing the ability of senior executives to achieve business goals by using external mentors. The context is therefore different from counselling, where the individual's personal needs are central, and from much internal mentoring, where the primary goal is the passing on of values, knowledge, styles and skills. Internal mentoring is well suited to developing people within the existing culture and according to existing norms. External mentoring is more suited to supporting the change to a new culture, helping the organization deliver its business vision, and developing levels of performance and behaviour beyond existing norms.

Mentoring framework

At the individual level, the benefits of being mentored vary widely depending on the particular needs, aspirations and situation of the mentee. The goal is typically to improve an individual's work performance. This tension between the current level of performance and the desired level provides one axis of the model

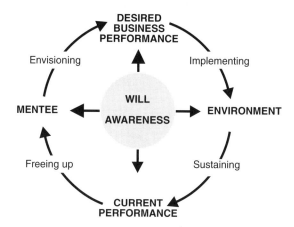

described here: the second axis is provided by the actions and behaviours that the individual takes into their work environment in working to achieve their desired level of performance, and by how they deal with the environment's response. (I am indebted to Danielle Roux and her Right Relations work for this framework.) The interaction of these two axes creates an approach to mentoring consisting of the following four elements: individuating, envisioning, implementing and integrating.

Freeing up

Individuating describes the process of developing autonomy, responsibility, and the ability to choose freely unconstrained by personal history. When working in this phase, the mentor's stance is nurturing and supportive and aims to help the mentee develop a strong positive self image. The basic question which the mentee seeks to answer in this phase is, *'Who am I?'*.

Envisioning

Envisioning is the process of connecting with a sense of purpose, identifying and choosing values, creating a compelling and stretching vision which is aligned to and supports the corporate vision, and committing to realising it. A key skill at this stage is the ability to create and hold a tension between the current reality and the vision. Without the ability to hold this tension, the vision merges with the current reality and merely reinforces the status quo. The mentor's role is to inspire the mentee and to help them answer the question, *'Where am I going?'*.

Implementing

Implementing consists of identifying the goals which will lead towards the vision, deciding on the strategies and actions to achieve these goals, and then taking action. The mentor's role here is to coach and to help the mentee answer the question, *'How will I achieve my vision?'*. This may include helping the mentee improve specific management skills in areas such as communication, team leading and time management.

Sustaining

Sustaining is the process of getting feedback from the environment about what is being achieved and the extent to which the vision is being realized, and its achievement sustained. When the mentee is able to see clearly what they are creating and to take responsibility for both their successes and failures, then there is the opportunity to learn from experience and gain insight into the changes necessary to deliver and expand their achievement of their vision. The role of the mentor is to challenge the mentee to see clearly the impact of what they are doing and to help them answer the question, *'Am I creating my vision?'*. Underpinning the whole mentoring process are two key skills — the ability to be self aware and the ability to exercise will. The development of these two skills provides the underlying context for the mentoring process and the degree to which the mentee enhances these two skills is one of the best indicators of the extent to which the mentoring process has created lasting changes in the mentee's effectiveness.

Experience has shown that executives can readily understand this framework, that it provides a meaningful way to think of their own change process, and that it reflects their experience of the mentoring process.

Issue 12 Spring 1996

III

Dynamics of Relationships

While organizations are keen to build good relationships with customers, it is also recognized that the emotions of employees are an inherent factor to maintaining organizational health. This section focuses on the nature of personalities, their influence on the organizational infrastructure, and some of the challenges such as Post-Traumatic Stress Disorder, Addictions and Bullying which have implications for individuals and organizations alike. The coping strategies for managing difficult situations and the context of new legislation widens the view into how comprehensive and flexible the provision of a counselling service can be.

The Essential Oil of Communication

Wendy Tobitt

*A company has a broad range of stakeholders and communication
is the key to productive relationships. Two-way communications
between employers and employees are especially important.*

At work and in our social communities we share a sense of common purpose and develop relationships by communicating with each other. The quality of those relationships contributes to the achievement of business and personal goals. Communication is the essential oil of organizations, and without it not only will relationships between people not grow and develop successfully but neither will the organization. For individuals, the stimulus of communication is as essential as oxygen is to survive. Relationships—and the communication which enables them—are at the core of successful organizations according to the report *Tomorrow's Company: The role of business in a changing world* which was published following a three-year inquiry. The inquiry identified five key relationships at the heart of every company: with shareholders, customers, employees, suppliers and with the community in which it operates at local, national or international level. The conclusion of the inquiry was that the secret of sustainable success lies in ensuring that the company derives the maximum value from each of these relationships.

Sir Anthony Cleaver, chairman of AEA Technology plc who chaired the inquiry, spoke of the communications issue at an Institute of Public Relations annual conference. He said that the inquiry found there was 'a lack of serious consideration at board level of the company's relationships with its key audiences and very little strategic consideration of how all five relationships should be managed, and a corresponding lack of measurement'. Sir Anthony explained, 'We felt that what was needed was a new language of success to enable the proper dialogue with all the stakeholders. Investors want returns on their risk, customers want affordable quality products and service, employees want satisfying careers and an affinity with the company and its values; suppliers want to be seen as valued partners; and communities want to see companies adding value to their lives.'

At the same conference, Jane Bufton of the University of Bath said, 'The staff, the people who work in an organization, should be seen as the body corporate—the trunk—of the organization because they invest so much more than the shareholders. They have a personal investment which motivates them to get up and go to work each day, and encourages them to do their job well. They must be more important than the City and shareholders.'

The *Tomorrow's Company* report speaks clearly to executives and directors about the benefits of successfully managing a business in a sustainable way, and encourages organizations to develop their own policies for greater commercial competitiveness within the framework of the five key relationships. However, there is evidence to suggest that not enough people and organizations are yet taking communication seriously.

The BT Forum was set up to research why communication matters and to provide the stimulus to encourage effective communication in the workplace, at home, within schools and the family. Through a series of roadshows and meetings, the BT Forum's Communication at Work and Home project spent a year listening to people speak about their relationships at work, and the work and home balance issues. The project team learned that:

- achieving a balance between work and home is still an issue for most
- the work environment needs to adapt and change to sustain open communication
- people feel ill-equipped to cope with the communication challenges at home and at work
- talking about work at home, and about home at work, is still taboo in each environment for many people.

The research shows that communications and counselling skills are required urgently in the workplace. The project is continuing with research into the effects of technology, demographics and employment trends on how we communicate in our personal and professional lives.

Employees are the key

Since communication through dialogue is essential to enable the five key relationships to develop successfully, communications with employees must be the key to unlocking the other four relationships. Employees are now frequently shareholders too; they are at least internal customers and may also be consumers of the company's products and services; they establish and develop relationships with suppliers; and they often live in the community in which the company is situated.

From my own work as a communications specialist I know how development of communications skills can enable people to feel better about their work, and for the company to feel the commercial benefit. This was demonstrated when working with a newly privatized company which was having to adapt to meet the changing demands of its customers. By listening to people, I learned how they communicate at work, and the impact this had on their relationships. Then by working with teams and individuals the process of effective two-way communication was developed. In this instance at the workshops with groups of blue-collar workers (who traditionally in most organizations do not have the opportunity to undertake such training), participants were encouraged to develop and use personal communication skills such as active listening, use of clarifying questions, non-judgmental responses, giving feedback and developing empathy.

The benefits were immediate, and this encouragement nourished their feelings of self-worth, improved their levels of trust and respect for their colleagues, and increased two-way communications in the workplace. The impact of this had a positive knock-on effect in the work environment and company culture. While those benefits for people in the immediate workplace environment are tangible, these will also be assessed qualitatively over 12 months through attitude surveys and other research. The company's benefits may take a little longer to come through in, for example, increased revenue and improved perception among customers, thereby leading to repeat business.

Clearly, a workforce enjoying better relationships with each other is more productive and beneficial for each of the *Tomorrow's Company* five key audiences rather than one in conflict. If the *Tomorrow's Company* report and the findings of the BT Forum research are to be taken seriously, then all of us as communicators will want to use these and other reports and projects in order to make the business case for counselling in the workplace and improved communications processes.

We know that counselling and communication skills can enable those relationships to grow and develop based on dialogue and trust. We also know that we have the skills and expertise to convince companies that there are real commercial and personal benefits to be gained from using our services. Let us take the opportunity to prove that communication is the essential oil of relationships and successful business. ●

Issue 15 Winter 1996

Facilitating Teamwork

Robert Nicodemus

It is important to understand the influence of personality at work,
and how differing personality styles can either add to or detract
from the process of effective teamworking.

How you try to facilitate the work of a team will depend in part on who you are in the team. A team leader organizes the agenda before a meeting and then encourages members to follow it, focusing on the task, making decisions and taking action. A leader may find that appeals to reason or authority are sometimes not enough to prevent or solve a problem which develops. Members of a team may often be effective in supporting the progress of work, but at other times no one seems able to help. Although some conflicts need to be allowed to work themselves out, they still need to be understood. Too often personalities and ideology seem to be the reason for difficulties which, in fact, may arise outside a team.

A team leader may be competent and prepared, but still seem ineffective in managing the team at some point, often early in the team's life. To avoid loss of confidence, a team needs to be able to make sense of an apparent loss of ability. One perspective is to think of the leader as working at the boundary of the team, negotiating relationships with the institution—an important, positive function. In that position, however, the leader may sometimes be perceived as a focus for anxieties which may actually follow the progress of work. Will the institution provide the resources necessary to do the work? Will the work be successful, or criticized when finished? What use will others make of the work?

The leader provides a focus for many mixed feelings about the hopes and worries of teamwork. She or he may represent important colleagues who are not members of the team. Worries about these distant relationships may be clarified and resolved by team members being able to make use of each other in ways which seem opposed to work, but which are important to working together. Any member may be caught up in these tension-solving activities, as may others outside the team—especially those with management responsibilities. Some worries have to do with relationships outside a team. They may at first seem vague and generalized but at the same time very stressful. As stress becomes focused through conflict or resistance to co-operation, it can also contribute to the quality and creativity of work because team members question what is going on, imagine and try out answers.

Taking responsibility

The management of an institution does have some responsibility to see that staff training helps team members understand the challenging process which occurs in all groups, especially what can be learned about the difficulty of the work and its impact outside the institution. It will be hard to find the time and space in a team when it is working to enquire into what is going on and why it is important. Making a commitment to learning about group processes on the job is even more difficult at the institutional level, between teams and the upper levels of management. Members of a team may be caught up in stressful processes, and the larger the number involved the more difficult it will be to think clearly. A person trained in counselling skills can be brought in to facilitate the processes, becoming a focus of ambivalent feelings that a team leader or members may experience. A consultant has no investment in the work or the outcomes, and may be freer to offer interpretations about difficulties in teamwork, providing a model for thinking which team members can take up in a realistic way.

A great challenge in facilitating teamwork is being able to take risks, especially where tensions become focused on personal issues such as gender, class, age, ethnic origins or religion. The ability to bring together in one place the creative and destructive processes in teamwork requires some acceptance of what cannot be known, understood or controlled. Although such beliefs may seem contrary to a technological world, they leave room for something of value beyond and outside one's self, team or institution. In that space may be room for ideas or people who are separate and different, yet part of a team. To survive in that space people need to trust their own feelings, especially when vague and unfocused.

A member of an institution is often best placed to provide support for teamwork but taking up a role of internal consultancy may require training as well as support. Maintaining the tensions so they may be examined and not avoided will be the greatest long-term challenge.

Issue 4 Winter 1993

What is Personality and Why does it Matter?

Beverly Steffert

The author introduces Belbin's 16 personality factors and indicates how managers and counsellors can use these insights to enhance their understanding of workplace dynamics.

*H*ow important is personality at work? Does it get in the way of smooth group work, productivity and creative project management? What is the famous 'personality clash' and how can it be resolved? Some of the more obvious temperamental dimensions are certainly important. Anxious, emotionally unstable and changeable people in the workplace can be a drain unless they are in a team that can use the positive aspects of anxiety and compensate for the negative. This was Belbin's (1981) insight about team 'roles'. When people are matched in their styles, roles and personality traits, they can cover for deficiencies and use strengths creatively.

A definition of a team is a group or people who share common objectives and who need to work together to achieve them. As any family member knows, the ideal and the reality rarely meet but unlike most family members, team members can be carefully selected for temperament, ability, experience and a team role which balances others on the team. This is what Belbin attempted to do using the personality traits identified by the 16PF (personality factors). Cattell's questionnaire is widely used in the workplace and the personality profiles generated have been matched to success, or otherwise, in occupations. Particular profiles have been show to be suitable for salespeople, military cadets, social workers, entrepreneurs, constables, executives, industrial supervisors, athletes, accountants and many others. One advantage of the 16PF is that is measures ability as well as reasoning, which is included in occupational fit. It correlates with the Work Motivation Inventory which measures the hierarchy of needs as perceived by Maslow. It is scored on the self-perception of the individual, even if the questions are not easily relatable by the individual to the global factors that he or she will eventually be judged on.

Most major decisions in organizations are made by teams, and team-building is an essential part of training courses offered by Employee Assistance Programmes. Social dynamics would predict that as certain roles are called for in a team, people fit into whatever role is necessary to interact appropriately with other roles in the group structure. Social expectation cues the reaction of others. If you need proposers, developers, delegators, advisors, cementers, opposers, everyone will sort themselves out into a best-fit team that can operate optimally. But in the real workplace people are quite aware that the right mix of people in terms of ability, preference and predisposition can create efficient, effective and contented teams, whereas the wrong mix can have disastrous results which are called personality clashes.

Key roles

Belbin is one of the few writers to recognize that personality can make a winning team or an unbalanced, dissident, unproductive one. He developed by observation, eight key team roles that he considered would make the most of the skills of various personalities, so that each can act as a resource for the others. These are:

Team Leaders:	Chairperson, Shaper
Creative thinkers:	Plant, Monitor evaluator
Negotiators:	Resource investigator, Team worker
Company workers:	Company workers, Completer Finisher.

So, making a winning team is a psychometrically sophisticated enterprise using people's own conceptions of their personality. Part of the team-builder's job is to lead people into awareness of participant's interactional skills. This clarification allows them to more easily identify what is going wrong when the team is stuck, at daggers drawn, all falling asleep or going down the wrong avenue with reckless abandon. These things happen in mismatched teams. If Belbin's observations are correct then building teams on personality factors most likely to fulfil the eight roles should make for a winning team, better than 'whoever happens to be there', or other degrees of imbalance. The very diversity of roles increases effectiveness by itself. Careful selection and design of teams might produce a champion racehorse rather than the proverbial camel. A good team can sense it's own faults and compensate for its team role weaknesses. The greater the spread of abilities in the team of course, the easier it is to do this. An excellent team is also sensitive to competition for particular roles because where such a situation exists there is what is called (inadequately) a personality clash, where two team members work against each other in competing for a role. Being aware of this possibility the team can work out how the role could be shared or reallocated.

Their skills were related to the 16PF by Belbin and others at the Henley School of Management and described in their much reprinted book *Management*

Teams: Why they succeed or fail (1984). ASE has since published *The analysis of personality in research and assessment* (1988) which describes further refinements of building effective teams using the 16PF, and their seminars are geared towards asking what personality characteristics does a person report that also tend to be reported by the individuals that fulfil particular team roles. This implies of course an understanding of how other individuals may be prevented from fulfilling their preferred team roles, by others who are 'competing' for it.

For those unfamiliar with the 16PF the meaning of the overall traits are outlined below:

Warmth:	emotionally distant ↔ attentive, warm to others
Reasoning:	ability to solve problems using reasoning
Emotional Stability:	feelings about coping with day-to-day life/challenges
Dominance:	tendency to exert ones will over others rather than accommodating the wishes of others
Liveliness:	serious, cautious, careful ↔ animated spontaneous
Rule Consciousness:	willingness to accept and follow externally imposed rules of conduct
Social Boldness:	degree to which the person feels at ease in social situations
Sensitivity:	objective, unsentimental ↔ suspicion, sceptical, wary
Abstractedness:	practical, solution-oriented ↔ idea-oriented, theoretic
Privateness:	forthright, straightforward ↔ discreet, non-disclosing
Apprehension:	self-assured, unworried ↔ self-doubting, self-critical
Openness to change:	degree to which person makes own choices and decisions independently of the group
Perfectionism:	tolerates disorder, flexible ↔ self-discipline, organized
Tension:	relaxed, placid, patient ↔ tense, impatient, driven, hi-energy.

There are also global factors of: extroversion, anxiety, tough mindedness, independence and self-control. So workplace counsellors for example could find it useful to not only apply these personality insights to their own role in an organizational team, but also to their clients where dissatisfaction with work is cited as an issue.

The mathematics of matching combinations of personality scores to ideal team roles needs an accountant or at least a calculator but if you have neither, a software profiling programme is available which scores instantly and accurately the individual's potential to develop particular roles. ●

Issue 6 Autumn 1994

Stepping into the Wave

Susan Clayton

*All too often, a company will look only at the 'business process'
when things seem to be going wrong. Gestalt shows a way of
addressing how individuals influence organizational culture.*

The concept of the 'business process' has revolutionized the way organizations carry out their business in the last few years. It concentrates on identifying the workflows in the organization. There is, however, another side to business. This is about the people working in the organization: the human systems, the organization culture, 'how people get things done around here', team dynamics, power games, etc. All this arises from 'personal process' which lies at the core of counselling work. Personal process is the flow of an individual's inner experiences and behaviour. The concept as I describe it here comes from Gestalt, a discipline currently making significant contributions to organizations in Europe and now gaining ground in this country. This article introduces process counselling as a powerful way of counselling at work and adds a contribution to developing effective human systems. I will give examples on how personal processes can malfunction, and how they can be dealt with by the counsellor.

In organizations and management systems, we have traditionally focused on the task (business processes), having paid much less attention to personal process. So when organizations are ineffective, they tend to do the same again, they try to improve the way they do the task. This pattern of working does not encourage staff to look at how they interact and deal with dysfunctional relationships that interrupt the flow of human systems. Eventually these dysfunctions become too great and counsellors are called in to help. Using the concept of personal process, individuals and groups are helped to achieve a result in the way that is best for them. Counselling then includes educating clients to understand the meaning of personal process and to be aware of it in their work and in their lives. In so doing, the process counsellor avoids colluding with the task focus and begins to meet a fundamental need of the organization.

Personal process is what generates the behaviour of an individual. It can

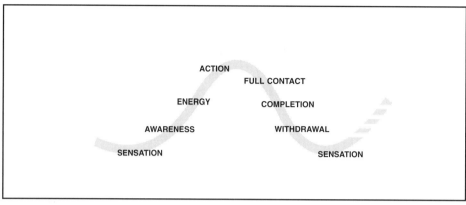

determine the level of interest or disinterest, the amount of energy given to a task, the impetus with which action is taken. Personal process is what makes people 'tick'. The diagram describes a wave (sometimes shown as a cycle), through which we can understand personal process in a single event or interaction. The key phases are shown below.

Sensation—Awareness: Sensation is the beginning of a process, the first sign of a wave emerging, the rising up of feelings, emotions, and needs. Awareness is our attention to sensations (self-awareness) and of our observations of the world around us (objective awareness).

Awareness—Energy: As we make sense of our experience we become excited, motivated, fascinated, driven, bored, frustrated, etc. All of these provide the energy to move forward.

Energy—Action: The phase from energy to action is about decision making, what action to take, what options are available. This is like the energy pushing forward in a rising wave.

Action—Full Contact: This is about 'riding the wave', staying in full contact with that energy point just beyond the tip of the wave. It is about staying with the action, not losing touch with it.

Full Contact—Completion: Here we learn, giving praise and recognition for our and others' achievements, offering and receiving feedback, discovering how we could do it better next time.

Completion—Withdrawal: This is the phase of letting go, feeling satisfied and ready to move on. The wave describes the way we make contact with ourselves, with others and the environment. For example, when interacting with another person the greater the contact the richer and more fulfilling the outcome is likely to be. This is because such things as hidden agendas and mis-perceptions are surfaced and discussed, and do not block the flow of the interaction. The process counsellor works with this flow, noticing the interruptions and blocks, articulating their observations to the client as awareness raising interventions. There are three key dimensions for the counsellor to work with:

- the blocks that interrupt the flow
- to surface and seek ways of dealing with unfinished business
- to build up wave skills (i.e. completion—where a client feels that they are not recognized and appreciated, the counsellor will encourage the client to be active rather than passive in meeting this need and to listen well to the feedback that they do receive).

Typical interruptions include:

- the client acting on assumptions or prejudices
- the client feeling inhibited or intimidated by other people, systems, etc.
- the client operating to fixed beliefs, views or rigid patterns of behaviour
- the client avoiding personal difference (i.e. always agreeing with what others say)
- the client ignoring what is being said for fear of hearing the truth (i.e. diverting the discussion onto something else).

You will notice that these are all processes, requiring observation or process interventions as opposed to diagnostic input. The counsellor is not dealing with the task (the problem being aired) but constantly and consistently working with the process. This is important, as to work with the task is to collude with the old familiar patterns that get in the way in the workplace. Bringing new ways of working into the picture becomes educational.

Building the wave

Building is about educating, bringing to the attention of the client their own capacity to develop themselves and to take risks in the workplace in order to grow. The five key areas below offer a wide range of topics to educate clients. They are linked to the phases in the wave. This then suggests that the counsellor's role is not just dealing with symptoms but approaching the core of many personal problems—education in personal and interactive processes.

These five areas are:

- raising awareness
- tapping into energy, creativity, inspiration, potential
- improvement through reflection and learning
- dealing with unfinished business
- identifying patterns of behaviour that seek to complete the unfinished.

Counselling style

Your influence and impact as a counsellor is dependent on your awareness of your own process. There is a term for this known as presence. This means bringing your own humanness into the counselling relationship and having the ability to 'bracket off' your own deep issues that are sensitive to the client's work. The more present you are the more effective you will be as a counsellor. Your role is in focusing on process issues, keeping task in the background, accessible if needed. The potential for the other person to learn and discover the way forward is dependent on your active process interventions.

Intervention strategies

The variety of process interventions are endless and dependent on the interpersonal dynamics that emerge from your meeting with the client and your own style of working. The following will provide some indication of the wide range available to you:

Diagnostic searching /questioning—'I'm not sure what it is you are trying to achieve'.

Experiential—'Imagine that your team are here in the room, what would they say about your suggestions?'

Metaphorical—'what sort of image does that conjure up for you ?' or 'the image I have is ...', or get them to draw a picture.

Confrontational—'You seem to be skirting around the subject, I'm not sure that you are giving me the whole picture'.

Conceptual—putting a woolly discussion into a clear conceptual framework.

Structural—suggest moving to a different room or different seats.

Experimental—working from a point of 'what if '.

Modelling—You model a way of working that will educate the client.

There are many psychological layers which you could intervene at; between conventional interventions (i.e. 'You seem hesitant') to the more risky, but often more engaging intervention (i.e. 'I'm confused and I notice that every time I ask, you change the subject'). Both are process interventions, and they are different—leading to different outcomes. The level of your intervention can only be assessed by yourself at the time.

The Wave is a very creative and empowering process for counsellors to work with, drawing on your own personal style and strengths for effective counselling. Above all it steps outside of the 'task' culture into the fluidity of personal processes and human systems.

Issue 11 Winter 1995

Company Values v. Public Profile

Lynn Macwhinnie

All organizations are keen to project positive public images as a marketing strategy, yet this will not work in the long term if it does not accurately reflect the internal culture.

An energetic organization implies dynamism, enthusiasm, vibrancy and assertiveness—all perceived as positive qualities as companies jostle for their piece of the pie in the marketplace. In recent years, there has been a change of tack for companies advertising their products. Instead of 'buy our beans because they are the best' approach, there is increasing use of 'buy our beans because we care about what you, the customer, cares about'. A few companies, such as Virgin and The Body Shop, pioneered this approach long before it was considered fashionable or even good business sense. Their profit margins have apparently persuaded other organizations to emulate their methods.

While this may be a cynical marketing ploy on the part of some companies, it nonetheless must have an effect on the energy and commitment of employees. They are galvanized by one means or another to be enthused and motivated by changes to an organization's public face. Mission statements (note the evangelical connotation) are redefined and repackaged. Excerpts are often displayed prominently in retail outlets and in publicity materials. For a company to be perceived as caring by the purchasing public is, therefore, deemed essential if financial success is to be achieved. The energy and enthusiasm of the chief, whether managing director, CEO, college principal or senior government official, has to inspire employees to light the touch paper of willingness within the organization to reflect this in public:' My company cares, therefore it cares about me, and I care about it.' Whatever collective focus there is for a company, the energy of the imagination, inspiration and intuition of all its employees needs space to flourish productively. Energy by its very nature is intangible and yet it is palpable in the culture of an organization. Note the difference between the atmosphere of a City bank and a social security office dealing with excessive demands on limited resources. Stagnant or depleted energy does not encourage even the most loyal employee to feel motivated in such an environment. The quality of the energy of the organization is mirrored in its employees and vice versa.

Organizations are often likened to families—preferably happy. Like many families, however, what goes on behind closed doors can be an entirely different matter. There may be internal rivalries and fears. Employees may not feel comfortable with the discrepancies they perceive between the projected public face and their own experience of the values within the organization. If employees do not feel valued, then changes are more likely to be met with suspicion rather than unqualified trust. If a workplace counselling programme is in place, however, then an employee can address the issues concerning them which may have more bearing on their personal past than their current employment. An illustration of this is the differing perception of whether a paternalistic company represents the 'caring parent' or the 'controlling parent' and the buttons that may push for the employee. Left unaddressed, such internal conflict can manifest in external behaviours incongruent with the company's public image. In counselling terms, dissonance is occurring. This fissure in an organization can have significant ramifications for the company which does not value its employees' pastoral well-being.

Energy is dynamic and generates and stimulates its likeness in the environment it is contained in. Company success must be measured against all the components which contribute to this energy. This includes employees as well as products or services, customers and shareholders. A public relations exercise will ultimately not be enough if, behind the scenes, there is not a collective weight of employees who know they are valued.

Issue 5 Summer 1994

Bullying at Work

──────────

Andrea Adams

Bullying is often difficult to identify, particularly when it has an acceptable face as part of a company's culture. It will often need to be dealt with at both the corporate and the individual level.

*B*eing bullied can reduce people, whatever their professional status, to the state of frightened children, by an experience they thought they had seen the last of when they left school. As it says in the *Talmud,* 'you can kill a person only once, but when you humiliate him, you kill him many times over'. As counsellors, you have a tremendously important role in being able to offer sympathy and understanding to the men and women experiencing what has been identified as more crippling than all the work-related stresses put together. Talking, in confidence, will help them to relieve their intolerable stress. Certainly, it is the unpredictability of these personal and professional attacks that causes the fear people feel. What is this psychological terrorization or, quite simply, bullying at work? In this context, it is the misuse of power or position to persistently criticize and condemn; to openly humiliate and professionally undermine an individual's professional ability until that person becomes so fearful that their confidence crumbles and they lose belief in themselves. These attacks on the individual are sudden, irrational, unpredictable and usually unfair. Despite this, bullying at work is still perceived in many organizations as 'effective management' which gets the required results.

Lack of awareness

Part of the problem is a lack of awareness, because of what bullying is usually called within organizations. Examples of this are: harassment, personality clash (a favourite euphemism), bad people management, intimidation, victimization, unreasonable behaviour, bad attitude, autocratic management, even working in a 'funny' way. Bullies are nearly always very hands-on people, who hover and breathe down your neck, like a bird of prey waiting for a distant mouse to twitch. When they pounce, they tend to pick on trivial matters and have irrational explosive outbursts. Bullying is often based on personal envy of a quality the bully does not possess. This can be a constant reminder of how they would like to be and are not.

Bullies are often tense and angry people who tend to manage by punishment rather than reward. The more overt tactics are the constant shouting to get things done; the appalling language and the jabbing of the index finger, usually when blaming everyone but themselves. It is often the unseen acts of aggression that make bullying more difficult to identify, such as setting objectives with impossible deadlines; removing areas of responsibility and inflicting menial tasks instead; constantly changing working guidelines, setting people up to fail; ignoring or excluding an individual; turning down leave for no apparent reason; blocking a person's promotion and spreading rumours to present someone in a dubious light. The physical symptoms for their target can include nightmares, insomnia, acute anxiety, depression, anger, loss of confidence and stomach and bowel problems.

Corporate responsibility

Bullies will often tell lies to cover their tracks and not trust anybody but themselves. Delegating, for them, means losing control. Those in the workplace who bully others may be effective in controlling their own fear, but they establish and maintain their power by creating fear in others, and that fear rapidly becomes infectious. Bullies could be described as 'victims on the run'. Due to experiences in earlier life, they are usually insecure people who are afraid of failing, of getting it wrong and being blamed. A lot of their behaviour is about self-defence; putting in a pre-emptive strike to ensure no-one else gets the better of them ever again. Yet the ethos of the workplace, and whether or not bullying is tolerated, is established from the top. If it is allowed to happen there, it will be passed down and seen as the acceptable way to manage.

The signs and symptoms which should persuade companies that this is an issue to take seriously include rising sickness and absenteeism rates, rapid staff turnover and inexplicable declines in profits and productivity. All the indications from four years of research show that bullying is endemic in many industries and organizations. Since empowerment appears to be a management buzzword for the 90s, recognition of this problem is essential if this sort of malicious ill-treatment is to be legitimately challenged. As Confucius said, 'To see what is right and not to do it is want of courage'. ●

Issue 1 Summer 1993

Healing the Impact of Bullying

Danielle Douglas

*Almost every type of discrimination falls under the banner of
bullying, and it demands the response of all the mechanisms
available to the workplace counsellor.*

here is a growing awareness in the business community of the extent to
which oppressive behaviour interferes with well-being, morale, motivation
and contribution to the job. Increasingly, it is becoming accepted that,
beyond their rights by virtue of the employment contract and health and safety
legislation, workers have a third right: to be treated with respect in their capacity
as human beings, thereby ensuring employee dignity. Misuse of power is a
serious behavioural issue. It takes the form of bullying (obsessively, as different
from the occasional spirited outburst), making unreasonable demands (moving
the goalposts, changing the deadlines), shouting and intimidating threats ('your
performance is inadequate, you will be disciplined', in a way that can not be
substantiated), marginalizing and isolating an individual, finding someone to
blame and making them the scapegoat.

The upshot for the recipient is persistent feelings of humiliation, loss of
self-worth, increase in stress and emotional distress, fear, anxiety culminating
in physical symptoms, and an inability to confront the bully for fear of reprisals.
Sometimes the individual will choose to leave their job because the pressure is
too much to take, or may become too ill to work as a result of stress and then be
dismissed on medical grounds with either a pension or medical severance
compensation. Those who have chosen to take their case through the legal
system have to cope with additional distress, and in many well-documented cases
long-term counselling has been necessary before the individual has recovered.

Oppressive behaviour generates inside the recipient a deep, not
necessarily conscious, wish for revenge and retribution, which is more often than
not suppressed. What motivates the bully is often not entirely dissimilar from
that which underpins the victim-type behaviour. At one time in their life, bullies
were victims too.

The Tavistock Clinic has given the following explanation for bullies:

'people who were constantly attacked for anything they did wrong as a child may use aggression as a form of self-defence in adult life, keeping others at a safe distance so that no one gets the better of them again. They may believe that as an adult they can get their revenge by giving others the experience they had as a child and were then powerless to stop, becoming very angry and intimidating towards others. When people do not behave as bullies want them to, they experience a feeling of impotence and that they are not the strong person they want to be. Bullies would regard anyone who is more popular, more efficient, or better qualified than them as absolutely intolerable.'

Reality in corporate life

As organizations restructure, rationalize and transform, become 'leaner and meaner' (meaner!?), the accompanying insecurity often generates more bullying behaviour. Also, the perception and tolerance level of harassment varies by industry sector and hierarchy and what can be seen as acceptable behaviour in one industry or hierarchical level might not be acceptable in another. Some organizations can acquire quite a tyrannical culture. Individual boundaries vary, and therefore what is acceptable banter in some circumstances for one person, may be totally intolerable behaviour for another. It is not so much the action in itself which constitutes bullying or harassment, but how it is perceived by the recipient. Unacceptable in any context are ways of behaving which are unwanted, obnoxious, make the workplace an intolerable place to be or affect an individual's career or job prospects. A person who is subjected to oppressive behaviour often shows signs of altered behaviour, such as becoming introvert, work showing a decline in quality, increased sickness absence, avoidance of work colleagues, or requesting a sudden transfer.

Legal trends

In law, it is now possible to seek redress for bullying behaviours which generate sufficient emotional distress and unhealthy physical stress. There are a number of sexual and racial harassment cases which fall within the scope of the Sex and Race Discrimination Acts, and other recent well publicized cases that have demonstrated where organizations have been in breach of providing reasonable duty of care, thereby being within the realm of the Health and Safety at Work Act. There is evidence that women raise bullying and harassment issues more readily than do men, who perhaps feel a threat to their masculinity and ration-alize it away by trying to behave in a 'manly' or 'macho' way. However, there is a growing trend in men complaining, particularly where racial abuse is involved. Relatively recently a lecturer won significant compensation after being the target of derogatory racial names from a colleague. The head of the educational establishment was made personally responsible for paying part of the compen-sation awarded at an Industrial Tribunal, the Commission for Racial Equality became involved and the case has gone to appeal.

Positive action

A wise organization will have a policy which ideally includes an option to resolve the problem informally, backed by counselling and mediation. This parallel option will exist alongside the formal complaints procedure. Encouraging those experiencing oppressive behaviour to come forward with complaints (or in some cases to even acknowledge it is happening to them) has been found to be counterproductive, as they fear the stigma and further retribution.

A good example of a supportive organizational response is that of South Yorkshire Police. They define harassment as '*any unwanted or hostile or offensive act, expression of derogatory statement, including incitement to commit such behaviour, which causes distress or affects the dignity of men and women at work*'. Their 'First Contact Scheme' is designed to provide a confidential listening service to support those who have experienced racial, sexual or personal harassment. They provide advice and guidance to restore confidence and raise self-esteem, to pursue an informal approach should the aggrieved so desire and to provide help and support to pursue a formal grievance. The range of options that will be considered include:

- that of the aggrieved person taking no action
- speaking to the equal opportunities advisor
- confronting the harasser
- invoking a grievance
- seeking the formal involvement of the disciplinary procedure
- considering external help.

The scheme exists to help the aggrieved person regain confidence and control. All of us working as counsellors know that policies and their implementation are often not enough. Experience suggests that helplines, help-desks, one-to-one counselling, employee assistance programmes and occupational health departments (where they exist) play a critical role in supporting those who have found their health and their personal and professional lives completely compromised due to the impact of bullying behaviour upon them. Support need not be limited to those aggrieved. One organization in giving notice of summary dismissal to the perpetrator of sexual harassment, also offered to pay for his counselling sessions. The reason was to ensure that he would not 'export' his behaviour to another organization.

Whilst an organization's last resort must be dismissal (irrespective of their position in the hierarchy), a mediating counsellor will look for a solution that is beneficial to both parties, arrived at in total confidence, non-punishing but healing, and which enables both parties to remain in employment in a dignified way. ●

Issue 15 Winter 1996

In-House Trauma Unit

Guy Harrington

London Transport staff experiencing PTSD are well met by their integrated in-house counselling service, which is also reflected in cost benefits to the organization.

The provision of London Transport's in-house counselling service to 18,000 employees requires both focus and balance. As with any service, the resources are limited and have to be focused in such a way that clients are afforded the opportunity to address and resolve issues, rather than receive generalized support providing temporary relief. The department strives to maintain a balance between the needs of the client and the needs of the business.

The department consists of three discrete areas: a Trauma Unit which combines research into and treatment of Post-Traumatic Stress Disorder (PTSD); a Drugs and Alcohol Advisory Service and a Generic Counselling Team. The aims of the counselling service are compatible with the goals and objectives of a commercial organization; the service maintains, increases and promotes employee psychological well-being and consequently helps to maximize productive employee working time and reduce company risk. The Trauma Unit is currently undertaking comparative research into three types of exposure-based therapeutic treatment or PTSD. They are Traumatic Incident Reduction (TIR); Eye-Movement Desensitization and Reprocessing (EMDR) and Direct Therapeutic Exposure (DTE).

Case study

An overview of the integrated service is best illustrated by the case of 'Peter', who works as a multi-functional station assistant. Peter was referred to the Generic Counselling Team after being physically assaulted by a customer. Peter had initially been absent from work for five days following the incident after which time, supposedly feeling fully recovered, he returned to work. Three weeks later, Peter started to experience nightmares and flashbacks connected to the event and he felt unable to deal with customers directly. He consulted his line manager who suggested he refer himself to the counselling service.

The generic counsellors use the initial session to undertake a structured assessment. This provides the counsellor with detailed information regarding the client's history but is also a useful aid to rapport-building. Following the assessment the counsellor decides with the client an appropriate course of action. Options include referral within the department or to external agencies; undertaking an initial six sessions of counselling or a consultation with the department social worker. It is the counsellor's responsibility to ensure that each aspect of the service is clearly explained, the purpose of the assessment procedure is understood and that the client experiences their needs as being individually attended to by the different practitioners in a holistic integrated way.

During the assessment session, Peter revealed that, prior to working for London Underground, he had served in the armed forces and had twice undertaken tours of duty in Northern Ireland where he was involved in a number of potentially traumatic incidents, including the shooting of his best friend. The counsellor observed a number of symptoms consistent with PTSD and decided to refer Peter to the trauma unit for further assessment.

Peter attended the Trauma Unit for a screening session with one of three counselling psychologists responsible for treatment. The screening involves a combination of psychometric tests and interview. During the screening, the practitioner became concerned in regard to Peter's alcohol consumption. These concerns were voiced to Peter and he acknowledged that he felt he 'had a serious problem with drink' and was consuming in excess of eight pints of lager a day. He related that his family had a history of alcoholism and his father had died as a result of alcohol abuse.

Resolving trauma

The Trauma Unit does not accept clients with chemical dependency issues as they are not able to engage with the treatment fully. The Drugs & Alcohol Advisory Service assessed Peter to be chemically dependent and arranged for him to attend a detox centre for two weeks followed by a further six weeks of residential treatment. The shortfall between the amount charged by the treatment centre and the amount paid by Peter's local authority was met by London Transport. After Peter had stopped drinking and completed residential treatment, his nightmares worsened and he began to experience flashbacks of various traumatic incidents on a daily basis. He returned to the Trauma Unit where he was randomly assigned to the Traumatic Incident Reduction (TIR) treatment group. TIR involves having the client silently review and then tell the counsellor about the trauma many times, until the trauma is no longer active. Sessions vary in length depending on progress.

The client can be asked questions to bring out the feelings they currently have and had at the time of the trauma. The counsellor does not interpret or evaluate the meaning but they help the client to find a personal meaning in the experience. A number of related traumas may be handled in the same session. Connections to earlier trauma are also examined and resolved.

Peter resolved his trauma after seven hours of session work and returned to work shortly before completing the TIR. He was retested and was judged to be no longer be suffering from PTSD. He will be recalled to the Unit at regular intervals over the next two years to ensure that he remains psychologically well. He now attends an aftercare group run by the Drugs and Alcohol Advisory Service and also individual sessions, the aim being to supplement the aftercare and monitoring service. He will continue to do this for a period of six months.

Peter is a very neat example, although unusual, of an individual who benefited from the full range of services offered by the department. Even the social worker became involved in the case and was instrumental in helping to re-house Peter away from his family home where, if he continued to stay, it was felt he would be at serious risk of relapsing.

Assessing value

The counselling service is being constantly developed in order to meet the needs of clients as effectively as possible. Trying to satisfy increasing demand with an appropriate balance between short-term counselling, longer-term therapy and external referrals is not an easy task but it is assisted by regular service evaluation. It can be difficult for a counselling service to demonstrate the benefit it contributes to business in empirical form but the pressure for services to do so is likely to increase. Workplace counsellors need not be afraid if our experience at London Transport is anything to go by. An evaluation of the Trauma Unit by independent 'number-crunchers' found that the Unit saved almost £400,000 in terms of sickness absence and other treatment costs in its first year of operation. As our service continues to develop we hope to contribute to the on-going debate in relation to PTSD and to the efficacy of general and workplace counselling.

Issue 16 Spring 1997

Putting Disability in the Picture

Susan Scott-Parker

This keynote speech at the 1997 ACW conference addressed the
spirit of the Disability Discrimination Act, and how best practice
can be encouraged by understanding and awareness.

Disability runs through everything you do. One in six people in any organization will be caring for someone who is disabled. People are routinely harassed and bullied on account of disability at work. As counsellors, you are dealing with people going through trauma such as being told they have multiple sclerosis, or who are dealing with mental health issues—sometimes called stress, but hardly ever called disability. We need to shift the whole tone of the debate on disability and promote a best practice culture, a spirit-based culture, rather than focusing on compliance with the legislation. In the old days, disability was a medical and charity issue and it was managed accordingly—the language was about needs, treatment and care. The new language is about rights, policies and litigation, and the emphasis is on policies. The old focus was about what was wrong with the person, the new focus is what is wrong with your policies.

Influencing policy

The Employers Forum on Disability (EFD)has 240 employers as members. We are the employers' organization that is focused on disability. Our members employ more than 17 percent of the workforce and includes organizations such as The Boots Company, The Post Office, Crown Prosecutors Office, BP, British Airways etc etc. We are a self-help group with a long track record of promoting best practice that long precedes any legislative debate. We help our members to promote strategic change, gain top team commitment and to get the information across about the business case for tackling disability.

One of the objections to the legislation is founded on most people's assumptions that we are talking about wheelchairs (thought being: 'we have to take the whole building apart in order to accommodate a disabled employee'), which builds up resistance even before you start. Actually, fewer than five percent of disabled people use wheelchairs. Getting that kind of basic fact across in a company can be very helpful. We are also here to influence government policy. We brought our members into the heart of the debate about the legislation, helping to shape the Code of Practice. It is all there and is the only guidance tribunals are obliged to look at. Our aim is not compliance with the legislation. We are about best practice, about why companies would have done this anyway, were doing it anyway and providing the tools and the information you need to drive it forward. We cover both the employment and the customer front.

The legislation protects customers from less favourable treatment. Over time it will compel anyone who provides goods and services to make reasonable adjustments to their premises or the way they operate, for disabled customers. In fact, you are covered by that legislation. All your offices will need, where possible, to be accessible, maybe they already are, but the point is that as a provider of a service you will be covered by the legislation. One in four customers are disabled or close to someone who is. Now this has proven to be a very powerful argument for capturing the attention of those areas of an organization that are not too wild about equal opportunity as a concept. From the beginning, we needed to challenge the kind of discomfort that people anticipate when they contemplate meeting people they reckon are somehow different.

Lack of understanding

One of our members, a huge bank, had this experience. A man applied for a job and put on the application form that he had had a kidney transplant and at the interview mentioned he had a hearing aid but could lip read with no problem. The interview goes along, finishes, not a single question about any of that. On the way to the lift the interviewer said, 'Well, how much time off do you need for kidney dialysis?', and he realized, through the whole interview, she had assumed he was off sick all the time. He said, 'Well that's why I had a transplant so I don't have time off'. Then he got the letter, no job, sorry, one of the reasons being he failed to make eye contact! There is nothing deeply prejudiced about that, it is just complete lack of awareness and a readiness to act on untested assumptions.

We campaigned for anti-discrimination legislation on the strength of the work we have done with members. We surveyed their views and it was very clear that the informed employer community in this country wanted legislation which would position disability on a par with race and gender, so it can be managed in the same way inside the organization. Most of British industry, however, does not really understand it. There is a lot of complacency out there and some hostility. Procedures are reviewed and it is the classic self-fulfilling comment, 'we don't get disabled applicants, it's not a problem for us' when of course the big issue is actually retention. Some 85 percent of litigation in America is linked to retention. It is the people working for you now who, if they become disabled, are most likely to be problematic in terms of industrial tribunals. Most of the cases going through are indeed just that.

'Psychic costs'

There are fears about the cost of policy implementation. Yet adjustments usually cost around £200-£300 on average and this year's Roebuck survey showed that most of them cost nothing. 'Access to work' is available for funding the extra costs associated; it could, for example, be for an interpreter, it does not just have to be funding for equipment. Actually, the financial costs are not the big issue, the real costs that we do not acknowledge are what in California they call 'psychic costs'. The costs of having to think differently, work differently, not being able to make assumptions, having to justify decisions you never had to justify before.

There is this deep-rooted assumption that to be disabled is not to be able to do things, by definition. It is not like race and gender, because 'you cannot have a blind bus driver, can you?' The communication job we have is to get people to say well you could have a blind bus driver if she had a valid driver's licence. It is the licence that counts. Now if we can get that across, we will have communicated all you really need to know about the legislation, and people will shift to looking at competencies.

A classic is the railway company in Canada that told me with great pride that they had a deaf person handling customer complaints on the phone. Now it sounds like a good way to handle customer complaints but the thing was that she could hear them due to a gizmo on the phone. Given the old way of looking at it, she would have been laughed out of the room when she applied.

The legislation is that it now makes it unlawful to treat disabled people less favourably than others on the grounds of their disability, and unlawful to fail to make reasonable adjustment. To justify less favourable treatment, an employer would have to show a material and substantial reason which cannot be resolved by a reasonable adjustment. So I would really try to get across to your colleagues that they must not assume they know anything about someone because of their label. Multiple Sclerosis does not tell you anything about the person. People with a severe stammer will be protected by this legislation. Most of your colleagues probably would not immediately think of as disabled those people with an impairment which may result, for example, from cancer, alcohol or drug abuse.

Heart of the legislation

The definition protects people who have been disabled in the past. These are people who at the moment are being refused a job because their medical history shows they were, for example, anorexic in the past or had severe depression. Now you have to produce evidence that this person, and their performance in the future, makes it impossible for you to anticipate making an adjustment which would be reasonable. Adjustments are the heart of this legislation—management systems, the policies, technical aids and equipment, and access to buildings.

We are not starting from scratch. Members were tackling this long before the Disability Discrimination Act loomed. We arranged with the Autistic Society to take a group of our members to meet people with Asperger Syndrome and to get some information about why they were not getting jobs despite their qualifications. Well, one chap was so excited by British Rail that instead of answering questions about the interview, he asked how the interviewer had arrived, what train he took and did it connect with the 6.42 and then did he move on to the 8.43. Now he is working at British Rail answering customer queries on the timetable for the trains because he memorizes the new timetable in one day. What we discovered was actually when you got the right job match that something quite exciting happened.

Issue 17 Summer 1997

What Every Counsellor Should Know about HIV Testing

Carolyn Walker

Updated to take account of changes in understanding about HIV and available services, this article gives useful background for counsellors who may be called upon to address these issues.

*I*f you were approached by a client with questions about HIV testing, how prepared would you be? Few illnesses generate such anxiety, fear and prejudice as AIDS (Acquired Immune Deficiency Syndrome) which is caused by the Human Immuno-deficiency Virus (HIV). Accurate information and sensitive understanding can help avoid many potential HIV-related problems in the workplace. At an organizational level employers can promote understanding by ensuring that an HIV policy and a staff training programme are in place. Workplace counsellors can familiarize themselves with basic information about HIV and the issues which arise in HIV counselling. One of the concerns which clients may present in counselling is whether to have an HIV test.

Clients may be contemplating an HIV test for a variety of reasons. They may be worried about the risk of infection through unsafe sexual or drug-taking activity, or perhaps through working practices which involve contact with body fluids or dirty needles. Sometimes a new sexual relationship or an unfaithful partner can trigger concerns. Proof of being HIV negative may be required for an insurance policy, travel visa or foreign work permit. Others may fear, realistically or otherwise, that their current health problems are HIV-related.

In the past, many people who suspected that they were HIV positive may have avoided testing, because it seemed that so little could be offered in terms of medical treatment. However, recent drug trials have raised hopes that early diagnosis and treatment with combinations of drugs can significantly delay the onset of HIV-related illness. This may motivate more people to seek testing sooner, rather than waiting until they develop symptoms. Another recent development is that many pregnant women are being offered the HIV test as part of routine ante-natal care. This is because early intervention can help prevent the virus being passed from an infected mother to her baby. In all these situations access to clear information in a confidential and non-judgemental atmosphere is paramount. The decision to be tested for HIV can have profound personal, social and practical consequences and should not be taken without pre-test counselling. Counselling offers an opportunity to consider the client's knowledge about HIV and AIDS, their risk of exposure to the virus and the personal implications of either a positive or negative test result. The primary aim of the counselling session is to ensure that fully informed consent can be given to testing.

For most people, the best place to have an HIV test is an NHS genito-urinary medicine clinic (GUM or STD clinic). Pre- and post-test counselling and high standards of confidentiality are offered by staff specially trained in HIV counselling and care. Clinics are listed in the local telephone directory and they do not require a GP referral. For workplace counsellors helping their clients explore their feelings about whether to go for an HIV test, the following pre-test counselling check-list may be useful:

Risk assessment

It can be helpful to start by exploring the client's main concerns about HIV and why he or she is considering being tested. Careful discussion can help to clarify the client's perception of his or her risk factors. Counsellors should guard against any tendency to prejudge whether a particular client seems likely to have been at risk. They also need to feel comfortable discussing 'social taboos' such as sexual practices, homosexuality, drug-taking and prostitution.

In order to assess accurately their degree of infection risk, clients need to know how HIV can and cannot be passed on. Transmission can occur when blood, semen or vaginal fluids from an infected person pass into another person's bloodstream. Therefore having unprotected sexual intercourse or sharing unsterilized drug-injecting equipment with someone who is HIV positive is a high risk activity. Infection can also follow medical treatment abroad in countries where unscreened blood, blood products or non-sterile instruments are used. And an infected woman can pass the virus to her baby during pregnancy, childbirth or breast feeding.

HIV cannot be spread through the air or in normal social contact, so there is no risk in the workplace from sharing toilet or canteen facilities. Standard hygiene procedures give protection to domestic and healthcare staff who may come into contact with body fluids or discarded needles. Information about HIV transmission can be clarified through discussion and any misconceptions clarified by the counsellor. Although some clients may appear well informed it is important not to assume adequate levels of understanding. Whether or not the client decides to have a test, pre-test counselling provides an important opportunity to clarify how to avoid acquiring HIV infection or passing it to others. This may include discussion about safer sex or safer drug use, or focusing on how to negotiate safer sex with a partner. How will being tested help the client? A negative test result can give peace of mind and reduce anxiety. A positive result can, despite the initial shock and distress, help a client take control of his or her life and make plans for the future. On the other hand many people still feel unable to face the overwhelming pressures associated with an HIV diagnosis whilst a cure remains to be found. The psychological and social consequences of HIV infection can be devastating: emotional trauma, personal rejection, social stigma and discrimination in employment, housing and even travel.

Anyone planning to be tested needs to consider this possibility, even if they feel that their risk is low. How do they feel they would cope and where could they seek support? Counselling can help to explore previous experiences of dealing with crisis situations. There may be concerns about the impact of a positive result on a partner, family or friends, or fears that disclosure at work could lead to discrimination or even dismissal. Clients may need help in deciding who to tell about their decision to go for a test. It is wise only to confide in those people who could be trusted if the result turned out to be positive.

Practical information about the test

Some GUM clinics now offer same-day testing, whilst at others the results take up to seven days. Most HIV tests involve taking a small blood sample and examining it for the presence of HIV antibodies. Antibodies take around three months to develop after infection occurs, so a test within this 'window period' will not detect a recent infection. A positive test result indicates that the person has been infected with HIV and can be infectious to others. It is not a test for AIDS. It is very important that clients understand the difference between HIV, the virus itself, and AIDS. Acquired Immune Deficiency Syndrome is the name given to a collection of medical conditions which may develop only after years of gradual damage to the immune system by the virus.

Supportive measures

Most clinics insist that results are given face to face, rather than over the telephone, and offer a post-test counselling session. When the result is negative this includes checking that the client understands the result and how to reduce the risk of future infection. Negative clients who remain at risk of infection and those who continue to feel highly anxious about HIV despite reassurances (the 'worried well') may benefit from further counselling at this stage. For clients who have tested HIV positive, the specialist team in a GUM clinic will offer further tests, a medical check-up and treatment if necessary. Clear factual information is essential for the newly diagnosed, including how to maximise good health, how to protect others from any infection risk and where to get good medical, practical and social support. Voluntary HIV services offer valuable contact with other HIV positive people through drop-in support groups and out-of hours telephone lines. Post-test counselling can help deal with the initial shock of the test result. Immediate reactions vary but may often include disbelief, fear, despair, anger, guilt and a profound sense of loss and grief.

Further counselling can be of immense value in the weeks and months following an HIV diagnosis. Indeed, a counsellor may one of the few people the client feels able to trust with the news that they are HIV positive. Feelings of isolation, secrecy and uncertainty are common at this time. Specific concerns may include how to tell others, fears about confidentiality, discrimination and rejection, and the 'dreaded issues' of disability, death and dying. Additional support may be needed during crisis periods such as starting a new sexual relationship, the onset of illness, beginning drug therapy or receiving an AIDS diagnosis.

HIV counselling can be stimulating and rewarding work but it can also be stressful. Feelings of inadequacy and hopelessness may be experienced by the counsellor as well as the client. Specialist HIV counsellors in local health or voluntary services can be a useful source of support and consultation. With good supervision and background knowledge about HIV counselling issues, non-specialist counsellors can offer support to their clients for whom HIV is a cause for concern.

Issue 7 Winter 1994

Detecting and Dealing with Depression

Lynn Macwhinnie

*Depression is recognized as an illness which demands being taken
seriously. It is up to organizations to recognize the symptoms early
and have appropriate support services in place.*

Many factors in the ongoing recession can easily exacerbate depression. Not that the current economic climate is the scapegoat for all our woes because, according to the Royal College of Psychiatrists, as many as 30 percent of the population will experience depression at some point in their lifetime. A recent survey has estimated the annual cost of depression to be in the region of £3.5 billion. This includes the cost of GP and community nursing care, hospital admissions as well as the financial impact of some 155 million working days lost. Not only is depression a common condition, it can also be so disabling that its effect on an individual's personal life, family and working environment can be devastating.

The myths of depression being equated with weakness and inadequacy are an unfortunate aspect of our cultural belief system and mental illness is, in some quarters, still a taboo subject. Hardly surprising that sufferers often hide their distress, sometimes with tragic consequences. Of the 5,000 people who commit suicide each year, 70 percent are suffering from depression. While the rate of suicide among women is significantly lower now than in the past, there has been a dramatic increase for men in the last ten years.

As part of a national five-year campaign to defeat depression, this last week has seen the issue highlighted in the media, with one day specifically focused on depression in the workplace. No doubt this has prompted many employers and employees to consider what this must mean to them and what they can implement now and do in the future. Although work has a largely beneficial impact on mental health, there are circumstances which can trigger an employee's depression. There are questions the organization needs to address, such as: is the employee working in isolation without support? Are the physical conditions cramped, poorly ventilated, noisy or badly lit? Has the redundancy procedure taken account of the feelings generated? Are the productivity demands unrealistic? Is there bullying in the office? Are an employee's skills equal to the task? Is fear an aspect of the organizational culture? The employer may be surprised by the responses.

Employees throughout a company need to learn to recognize the signs and symptoms of uncharacteristic behaviour such as tearfulness, an inability to concentrate, poor time-keeping, irritability, forgetfulness, low self-image and lack of motivation. Not only in others, but also in themselves. There needs to be an awareness of the situations in which people become most vulnerable to developing depression, for example redundancies, but also personal upheavals such as bereavement, divorce, illness and financial anxieties.

Implementing a counselling service

Due to government policies on mental health in the workplace, the onus is increasingly on employers to implement an appropriate policy as an integral aspect of the organization. With more companies being sued by employees for stress-related illnesses, the British Association of Insurers has some concern that the premiums will have to increase. The companies that have a employee counselling service will be able to show that they have made some efforts to meet their 'duty of care' towards their staff.

As with most common illnesses, recovery will be more rapid if treated in the early stages. Depression is no different. It is treatable. Most treatments fall into two main groups which are medication and talking treatments, such as counselling, and people often begin to feel better once they start talking about their problems to a trained counsellor. This is where an accessible and confidential counselling service in the workplace can make a significant difference to the employee whose coping strategies are no longer enough.

Complementary treatments

A major corporation in the USA has an EAP health plan which includes an option to employees of alternative or complementary support treatments. Encouragingly, as with counselling, these healthcare models are becoming more accepted in the UK as people experience their efficacy for their particular condition. As an adjunct to counselling, the use of other therapies, such as Shiatsu, massage, Bach Flower Remedies or homoeopathy, may be effective as part of depression treatment. They may be helpful in accessing unconscious feelings of anger, sadness and betrayal underlying the depression. Counselling is then utilized to develop awareness and appropriate coping mechanisms and to redefine personal boundaries. While people with depression can be supported with a variety of complementary treatments, the most suitable approach will depend upon the individual as well as the nature of the depression.

While the need to have strategies for dealing with illness is essential, we should not neglect to also focus on promoting well-being, an initiative which is already underway in the USA where the first Wellness Summit was held in Washington DC late last year (1993). A pro-active approach, which includes workplace counselling as a cornerstone of company policy, would do much to ameliorate any potential for accumulated problems manifesting in profound ill health—not forgetting the symbiosis of the organization and the employee. Healing also works both ways. ●

Issue 5 Spring 1994

Bereavement and Loss

Romey Chapman

Our embarrassment in the face of bereavement comes from knowing that nothing can retrieve the situation; honest action will, however, always be better than inaction or avoidance.

*I*n writing about a bereaved person in this article, I mean someone experiencing the loss of a significant other through death, although everything mentioned about that loss also applies to someone experiencing the end of a relationship through separation or divorce.

We all dread it the first time we have to face someone who has been bereaved. What are we going to do? What are we going to say? How are we going to resist the temptation to avoid the person and rationalize our cowardice? 'I could say the wrong thing, I might upset them and make things worse.' It is especially difficult to know what to say to someone at work, someone you may know only in that setting. There are so many factors to take into account, your position in relation to that person, whether it is a colleague, superior or subordinate, the nature of the relationship and to what extent you and the bereaved person have previously shared personal information. There is also the significance of the meaning of the loss. Has the person lost a spouse or an unacknowledged partner? The death of a grandmother may seem sad but timely to one person and come as a devastating blow to someone else. One person may experience the death of a pet as relatively insignificant while another will find it overwhelming. What is the person's own pattern of grieving? Grief is a universally experienced process but each person expresses it in their own unique way, influenced by a complex interweaving of cultural, religious, family and individual personal factors.

The first day back

People dread the first day back at work following the death. How are they going to face the looks, the whispers, over-cheerful greetings or awkward condolences? In a setting where coping and being in control are so important, what are they going to do if they cannot concentrate or remember things, if they feel so exhausted that they can barely get through the day or, worst of all, they are in a meeting and tears start flowing down their cheeks? 'I don't want people feeling sorry for me.' 'If anyone says anything kind I'm afraid I'll start crying'. 'Nobody said anything. It's as if they don't care'.

Once the shock of disbelief and numbness has worn off, the newly bereaved person experiences a see-saw of emotions. As Penelope Lively wrote in *Perfect Happiness*, '... *grief like illness is unstable; it ebbs and flows in tides, it steals away to a distance and then comes roaring back, it torments by deception. It plays games with time and reality.'*

The bereaved do not know from one minute to the next how they are going to feel or what they need or want. At the same time, they can be hard on others who fail to give them the *right* response. So what can colleagues do? How can they get it right? If you have lost someone close to you and you have experienced grief, you will know for yourself that almost anything is better than nothing. Bereaved people talk about the pain of seeing someone turn aside rather than face them in the passage, or make an excuse to get away quickly, or of having a conversation with someone who never acknowledges the loss. It is important to be real, not to take refuge in platitudes which tend to sound insincere or which minimize the loss like 'He's at peace now,' 'It must be a relief that it's over.'

Sylvia Townsend Warner wrote, '*I was grateful to you for your letter after Valentine's death, for you were the sole person who said that for pain and loneliness there is no cure. I suppose people have not the moral stamina to contemplate the idea of no cure, and to ease their uneasiness they trot out the most astonishing placebos. I was assured I would find consolation in writing, gardening, in tortoises, in tapestry ... in keeping bees, in social service ... and many of these consolers were people whom I had previously found quite rational'* (*Letters*, 1980).

A few words spoken honestly are what is needed: 'I'm so sorry. I don't know what else to say.' 'I've been thinking about you. How can I help?' It does not matter to the bereaved person if you look uncomfortable or the words come out awkwardly. It will mean all the more that you have made the effort in spite of your discomfort. Some people prefer to write the bereaved person a note, which may be more appropriate if you do not know the person well. These days it is a risky business to recommend physical contact but given a mutually acceptable context, a hand on someone's shoulder, a hug or a warm handshake can say more than words and bring more comfort.

Continued support

As the weeks and months go by, it is easy to forget a loss when it is not your own. But birthdays and anniversaries, a setback or an accident, a piece of music, another loss, illness, an unsolicited memory flashing into mind, can trigger grief off again. At work, people need a climate of continued support and understanding, someone who asks from time to time how they are and waits for the answer. Some people find their work a welcome and needed distraction, a way to hold on to their normality, and are able to hold their grief for private time. Others throw themselves into work to escape the pain and deny the reality of their loss. Grief which is suppressed can resurface over time in physical aches and pains, in a series of illnesses, depression and anxiety, phobias, drug and alcohol abuse. Unresolved loss may be hidden but it does not disappear.

In such situations, people may need professional help to enable them to work through their grief and come to terms with their loss. A trusted, knowledgeable colleague can play a valuable part in advocating the option of counselling. Workplace counsellors need to be alert to and explore the possibility of unresolved loss in their clients who often present with seemingly unrelated problems. In most situations, a few words, a listening ear and a climate of support and understanding can go a long way towards making it possible for a bereaved person to ease back into full productivity with the minimum of stress and difficulty.

Issue 9 Summer 1995

Wrestling the Octopus—Managing Addiction

Peter Steddon

*Substance abuse, including alcohol, is a challenging arena for
many counsellors, especially in the workplace, but there are a
number of ways of approaching the issues that usually underlie it.*

lients whose problems arise from, or are associated with or prolonged by, the use, misuse or abuse of alcohol or other over-the-counter, prescribed or controlled drugs can be unpopular with counsellors and other professionals. 'Hopeless', 'frustrating', and 'a waste of time' were some of the more restrained responses when I asked a group of experienced workplace counsellors for their honest reaction to working with such clients. And in recruiting for an international counselling network, I find that alcohol and drug problems top the list of 'pathologies' therapists prefer to avoid. Clearly, some of these professionals have had bruising experiences in the past which they are not keen to repeat. Possibly some of them were even attracted to the helping 'business' in the first place as an indirect result of experience with alcohol problems in their family of origin— in which case, it's entirely healthy to be in touch with what alcohol problem clients may represent for them.

But, aside from the possibility of unresolved personal issues for the professionals, are these problems really so difficult and dangerous? They can certainly be 'slippery': if you look back over the first sentence of this article, you will find four types of toxic substance, three types of use and three orders of consequences, offering many permutations—so that it's often not easy to 'get a handle' on the situation. 'Not easy' is a long way from 'impossible', however. These problems are treatable, and (please remember this) there is no such thing as a hopeless case.

Is it our problem anyway?

Employers can find many other ways to spend their money. Anyone who has ever tried will tell you it is not easy to persuade an organization to invest in preventive measures, and often there are cultural pressures against. On the other hand, employers pay most (over 85 percent) of the national bill for alcohol-induced social harm, so it is their problem more than anyone else's. Somehow we need to be able to find a way through the maze, because these problems are present in any workforce and if we ignore them, they are unlikely to go into spontaneous remission; on the contrary, they will probably get worse. One of the obstacles we face in trying to develop an effective response, is that efforts are divided: the few specialists in this field tend to be polarized into feuding camps, each not 'hearing' the other.

What is true?

Nobody knows for sure. Anyone who tells you otherwise is mistaken. When the neurologists can finally tell us exactly what every last piece of the brain is for and how it functions, we may be able to get closer to scientific answers. Until then, practitioners need to concentrate on what works.

What is useful?

What has been shown fairly convincingly is that an intervention is more likely to succeed if treatment can be matched accurately to the needs of each client. This means that we need to be able to make a careful assessment of the client's situation. The client needs to see that there is a problem and to want to do something about it. Knowing where the client is (in respect of drinking/drug use, awareness of it and motivation to change), is therefore more than half the battle. Many guidelines and diagnostic tests exist, including CAGE, MAST, SUDDS and SASSI. Most 'problem' drinkers/drug users are using at harmful levels, maybe in response to a life event or situation, and need to re-establish control. But the 80/20 rule applies: the far smaller number of addicted/dependent users causes most of the excitement. A pivotal question is, therefore, whether or not the client should be assessed as dependent/addicted, because (in my view) the problem then becomes different in kind, not just in degree, and you are up against a whole other dynamic. Face-valid tests, which ask questions such as, 'Have you ever … (lost a job, had an accident, been in a fight, etc.) because of your drinking?' can be expected to elicit a confident 'no' from dependent clients, because that is the client's reality.

Who is the client?

It may be the 'identified patient' but in the case of alcohol or other drug problems it is just as likely to be a spouse, child, line manager, union rep or co-worker, wanting to know what to do. Is the client in the room? It is often said that in Employee Assistance 'the client is the person in the room asking for help,' and most EAP clients are self-referred. But any workplace counselling service, whether internal or external, really has two clients: the employee/service user, and the employer who pays for the service.

Alcohol and other drug problems produce a regular crop of mandatory referrals by the employer for performance issues. In such cases, this second client relationship moves into the foreground, and all parties need to be quite clear about the subtle shift which has taken place.

What does the client see as the problem?

The answers may be very different, depending on who is identified as the client. The differences are important, but often not acknowledged:

- for the employer it is a performance problem, involving, for example, attendance, timekeeping, productivity, safety, interpersonal issues
- for a partner, it may be a financial problem (all the money goes on alcohol or drugs), or a domestic violence or legal problem
- for the 'patient', it may be about stress, unreasonable expectations at work, or a recent domestic event such as bereavement. Drinking or drugging is often seen as a response to those pressures.

What would be a successful outcome for the client?

Different formulations of the problem lead directly to different solutions:

- for the employer, the employee should probably stop/moderate the drinking or drugging and get performance back to an acceptable level as fast as possible
- for a partner, there should be an end to violence and other destructive behaviour, and a return to the way things were. A total end to drinking/drugging may not be desired
- for the 'patient', the goal may be to do whatever is necessary to protect a job or marriage, and get people 'off his or her back'.

How much of that can be achieved in the time available? Severe alcohol or drug problems are usually considered as long-term. EAPs and many other workplace counselling services offer a brief framework of say, three to eight sessions. We might conclude, then, that there is no point in trying but, at Alcohol Concern's annual conference, it was claimed that brief interventions do work. Steve De Shazer, originator of Solution-Focused Brief Therapy, also addresses alcohol and other drugs, though his method is more controversial.

Where to start?

For example, De Shazer states that alcohol (or drug) use is only a problem if the client says it is. (Not surprisingly, most clients do not.) His next question is, 'Is the person in the room a customer for anything else you can deliver?' For example, if the client identifies hassle from his line manager as the problem, the question becomes, 'What do we have to do to get your manager off your back so you don't have to come here any more?' Therapist and client may together conclude that to keep the boss happy it might be a smart move for the employee to do something about his drinking (even though it is not really a problem.) There are therefore different routes through the motivational interview but the aim is that the client be helped to see that 'change is necessary, change is possible, and change is your responsibility.'

What next?

For addicted or 'severely dependent' clients, it is likely that a counsellor will need to make an onward referral. It is, therefore, very important to have identified the options, and their funding implications, before the client interview. The problem in Britain is that service provision is so patchy. A big 'plus' for EAPs and other workplace counselling services in these situations is their ongoing contact with the client. If the first option fails, another can always be tried. Follow-up is important for this reason—and also because every client with a significant alcohol or drug problem is going to have a 'comet tail' of coexisting legal, financial, domestic and job-related problems, and will need the help of an EAP or workplace counsellor to avoid being overwhelmed by them. ●

Issue 15 Winter 1996

Addictive Organizations

Andrew Bull

Organizations can be addicts in the same way as individuals, and work itself can be an addiction. The lessons from Alcoholics Anonymous can be applied effectively in the workplace.

veryone has seen an alcoholic wandering around, dishevelled, talking to a can of lager. In fact, most people with problems of alcohol dependency are employed. This is not the only addiction, however, that is exhibited at work. Work itself can be an addiction. Schaef and Fassell[1] see it as belonging to the group of process addictions (addictions to on-going activities) like relationships and religions, and use the 12-step approach of Alcoholics Anonymous (AA). Like individuals, organizations can function as addicts. Organizational behaviour is said to mimic that of individual addicts. Diagnosis is based on observation of organizational behaviour, but this is not in itself sufficient. One also needs to look at how addictions develop in organizations.

Symptoms of addiction

Addicted individuals and organizations exhibit a number of symptoms, which include:

Denial—Issues are simply ignored or re-defined, such as when someone has had a strenuous day at the office, filled with conflict, and heads for the nearest pub with the rationale that they need to unwind.

Confusion—As within the family of an alcoholic, endless hours are poured into discussing exactly what is going on, when the next episode will happen and the best way to deal with it. The emotional atmosphere generated, the circular reasoning and the co-dependency of those in the addict's world ensures that confusion reigns.

Dishonesty—People addicted to work lie to themselves, to their immediate environment and to the world, e.g., never mind any internal differences, show the world we are united.

Perfectionism—This obsession remains an elusive goal, and the addict resorts to his/her 'fix' as a way of coping with unwanted feelings that result from imperfection.

Illusion of control—The addict tries to control the environment which, in turn, tries to control the addict. Both believe that unwanted thoughts, feelings and behaviours can be removed, the addict via the use of the addictive substance, and the environment via sanction or some sort of medicine.

Frozen feelings—Central to any addictive process is the use of substances to avoid unwanted feelings. Just as alcohol blots out emotion, work overcomes problems. All emotions become deviant and must be eradicated, even joy and excitement.

Work as addictive substance

Key people influence the way organizations function. For instance, I worked with a manager whose staff explained his workaholism as a compensation for the break-up of his marriage falling apart because of his slavish dependency on work. Not only did they collude by re-defining his problem but the norm for the department was to work long hours, thus normalizing his behaviour.

Work often becomes the addictive substance in organizations. It is central to the life of workaholics, it is their rationale for living. They define themselves and others through work, e.g., income, size of budget. Like any addictive substance, it holds out the hope of a bright future. Mission statements are good examples: future-oriented, inhabiting a world of excellence and completeness. The promised land must always be one step away, or the addict will be forced to confront one of their worst fears, the emptiness of their own existence.

Systems and structure

Addicted organizations and work addictions function within closed systems in which the range of permissible behaviour and thought is limited to those that reinforce the addiction. Addicted organizations lack responsiveness and growth is surrendered to survival. This calls for a defensive/aggressive attitude to employees, customers, products and markets. The organization tries to maintain the illusion of control and becomes autocratic, rigid and narrow in its focus. In its reluctance to accept reality, responsibility for problems is projected onto others. However, no system is ever truly closed and problems will arise which expose the dysfunction within the organization.

Thinking, decision-making and communication become dysfunctional. To reduce the risk of dealing with painful realities and unpleasant feelings, concerns are not communicated directly, but indirectly through memos, gossip and the use of intermediaries. Nor is skilled communication necessarily indicative of organizational health. For instance, news of a successful reorganization fails to reveal the increased likelihood of a take-over and more lay-offs. The addictive organization can also be identified through its structures as it sinks further into dysfunction, with bureaucracy proliferating. Guilt and blame become common emotional currency. Dishonesty culminates in disintegration as respect for the organization and others is lost. Employees leave, or costs associated with organizational stress rocket, such as absenteeism and poor production.

Managing addictions

Schaef and Fassell (ibid) write: 'because it is a whole system, partial recovery is not possible, for it is an entropic and destructive world-view that has taken over, not just a few bad habits'. Recovery, therefore, requires involvement of the whole organization, i.e. mission statement, products, structures and systems.

The disease model proposed by AA relies on organismic conceptualizations of organizations, e.g. systems theory. However, if organizations are construed as political systems, for example, a disease-based approach is redundant. The implication for the counsellor is that in the absence of concrete evidence as to the type of addiction/dysfunction and its cause, a metaphor must be employed to explain what is happening within the organization. As this will influence the problem focus and therapeutic strategy, the metaphor must be acceptable to the client organization. (See Morgan[2] for a discussion of metaphor as a way to understand organizations.)

This idea may be difficult to apply to large organizations because of conceptual and operational difficulties in defining the addiction and to whom or what it applies. It is easier to apply to small organizations/departments which are organized to collude with a key individual's dependencies. However, the notion of work as an addictive substance is worth taking seriously. ●

Issue 5 Summer 1994

References

1. Schaef, AW, and Fassell, D, *The Addictive organization,* Harper and Row, 1988.
2. Morgan, G, *Images of Organizations,* Sage, 1986.

IV

Creating Success

The successful organization is energetic with a vibrance that influences its wider environment. It has a distinctive culture which sets it apart from its competitors, who may occupy a very different place on the success continuum. For the workplace counsellor or practitioner of counselling skills, this requires a responsiveness that is appropriate to the prevailing culture. How flexible are counsellors? Are counselling's core qualities and values providing a seed bed for the emerging spirit-based workplace culture? Are counsellors modelling good practice in all their interactions? Authors in this section respond to facets of these questions with suggestions that may enhance both the organization and counselling at work. The brevity of this final section of the anthology indicates, perhaps, there is still significant room for exploration and growth—personal and professional.

Human Leadership and Counselling in Organizations

David Charles-Edwards

*The author suggests that transforming difficult work
relationships requires changing management styles and company
culture to a more humane and integrated model.*

*I*t is encouraging that the recognition of the place of counselling, EAPs and post-incident support is increasingly significant among employers. The perspective that there can be a deeper strength in acknowledging our vulnerability has begun to emerge. The growth of ACW, BAC and the Charter for Staff Support in the healthcare services are all signs of this new spirit. If we are interested in the health of organizations as well as people involved in them, we need to relate counselling skills to the way managers lead and not see them as primarily or even only relevant to the 'people people' in the company.

At one end of the spectrum, however, are managers who continue to cause a great deal of preventable and highly disabling stress. For example, a bright new macho manager called together all the engineers and their managers together for the first time after his appointment. Part of his message was that half of them would be out within a year, and it was up to each of them to decide whether or not they would be in that category. In another company, a new manager interviewed his key staff within a day or so of his arrival and asked each one which of their colleagues they would put on the top of the list for jettisoning.

The psychological brutality and insensitivity of these types of managers can and does occasionally trigger suicide and, often, abject misery and/or fury, which seeps back into family and community, leading to alienation from self and work. Training managers in counselling skills has profound implications for the way they lead all the time, even if ostensibly the focus of training is something where a counselling 'hat' is more easily accepted as in post-incident support or redundancy. The danger, however, is that if counselling skills training is out of harmony with the company's message about leadership, managers may become more inconsistent in their behaviour with the result that staff become confused or cynical.

Furthermore, any leadership model used in an oppressive organizational culture is likely to be used as a vehicle for, at best, colluding with unfairness; with the needs of the group and the individual being the focus of manipulation in pursuit of the holy grail of the 'bottom line'. Financial success or viability is essential to survival, whatever the organization, but the elevation of short-term profit as the sole criterion of success has led to the decadence of some companies, offering only the bleakest and most individualistic of inspiration to their staff. But experience and theory alike point to the growth of motivation in well led teams, towards factors that money on its own cannot buy.

Bridging the divide

The 1970s leadership development models introduced managers to the importance of process, which flowed naturally into an interest in workplace counselling. But we are still often left with a split, not in role, which is necessary and appropriate, but in values and skills. Line managers are concentrating on leadership (task, action, product understanding, discipline) and counsellors and occupational health specialists on human needs (process, understanding people, feelings, caring) with Human Resources and personnel people straddling the gap with varying degrees of discomfort. Such a split is dangerous even if at times it still seems unavoidable.

One bridge is formed by our understanding of motivation; to get the most from the human resource, we need to be energized and connected to how we feel. The whole-person approach offers another bridge in understanding how our behaviour at work is influenced by our feelings, values and beliefs. These in turn are affected by the whole of us—our past as well as our present, our life outside as well as at work, all our resources and the pressures on us. Good counselling may mean accepting the person; but equally it involves helping clients get tough on their dysfunctional patterns of thinking and behaviour, and ruthless in our determination not to collude.

The integrated approach implies, above all, an impact on the way leadership is seen. Such a commitment to leading humanly and humanely fits well with total quality and with participation and involvement. It also fits in with the need of companies to change from bureaucratic, hierarchical pyramids to more flexible, flatter, customer-centred organizations, in which power comes from skill, knowledge and influence more then position and status. Giving respect to people, irrespective of their place in the pecking order, is a prerequisite for respect from them to the company. The core conditions of helping are as relevant to good managerial practice as to counselling relationships. ●

Issue 1 Summer 1993

Integrated, Isolated or Irrelevant?

Michael Carroll

*At the 1997 ACW conference, counsellors were asked to review
their perspective on organizations, and consider how this will
influence their practice and thereby enable their clients.*

*T*here is a story told about a Sunday school teacher who asks her class: 'What small grey animal climbs trees, gathers nuts, and has a long bushy tail?' A little boy answers, 'I know the answer is supposed to be Jesus or God, but it sounds like a squirrel to me'. Workplace counsellors face that dilemma: do we give the answer expected of what counsellors and counselling should be (irrespective of the context) or do we trust ourselves, our workplace clients, the organizational contexts? Workplace counsellors sometimes seem to have the answers before they have asked the questions: it is relatively easy to become fundamentalist counsellors who believe all counselling answers are the same, no matter what the situation.

Sacrosanct rules

Ideally we learn how to do counselling and then adapt to the circumstances in which we find ourselves: Rogers put it well when he wrote, *'learn your theories well, but put them aside when you turn to meet your client.'* He was talking about adaptation, of client-centred work. What worried me in counselling training is that we teach sacrosanct rules and regulations that must be obeyed when your senses and your intuitions and your clients are dictating otherwise: we see squirrels and get anxious because we think we are expected to see Jesus or God. Have we made dogmas out of environmental rules? Are we creating counselling clones rather than adaptive, creative counsellors who would work with and around and through whatever their clients need, while maintaining professionalism, excellent quality and ethical stances? I think we may well become most integrated and relevant to organizations when we become corporate counsellors as well as individual counsellors.

People have all sorts of ideas of what a corporate counsellor is, becoming a consultant to the organization, a trainer of managers, taking over the HR function, etc. But maybe the answer lies in what we are already good at—counsellors of individuals. Our skills are:

- building therapeutic relationships which empower individuals to manage their own lives and decisions
- working with process skills which go beyond the immediate and obvious to isolate, understand and work with underlying dynamics
- dealing and working with emotions and the emotional side of life
- staying with pain as long as is needed. Good counsellors know how to stay with, work with and respect the pain of clients.

Are we creating counselling clones rather than adaptive, creative counsellors? If these are the skills we use best with individual clients, why do we not do the same with organizations? I listen to counsellors who do not apply to organizations, what they are excellent at with individuals. As they turn from the individual to meet the organization, they change:

- they become critical of the organization; faulting poor policy and bad management
- they move quickly to educate the organization, which is not something they do with their individual clients
- they fight the organization and take the side of the individual client against it. I am constantly surprised how many counsellors move into the organization as enemy to secure the rights of the individual
- they keep their distance from the organization, not getting too close in case they are contaminated
- they do not relate to the organization therapeutically but antagonistically
- they do not see the emotional side of the organization and the feelings which run rampant through it
- they do not see the pain within the organization as it tries to change, adapt, make adjustments, deal with transitions, implement redundancies and fight for its identity.

Change agendas

Perhaps we need to think of applying to organizations what we apply to individual clients—the same time, care, understanding, patience and, dare I say it, the same love. We suffer a lot these days from 'unloved organizations'. Perhaps a rule for those who would be corporate counsellors (or who work as counsellors within organizations) might be: do to the organization what you do to your clients. Do not go with your own agenda: with answers, or to educate, or to fight, or change the organization.

Might it not work if we were to accept, to understand, to be patient, to pace, to relate to, to work with, to challenge, to touch the emotions; to follow their agenda not our own. There are enough consultants around who know all the answers, without counsellors jumping on that bandwagon. The organizations

I work with are all in transition, and change and stress are part and parcel of their lives. They are organizations in pain, receiving little understanding or empathy (or sympathy), organizations which are constantly being criticised for not doing enough. Their problems are continually highlighted yet few solutions are offered.

Therapeutic relationships

Many people within organizations do not have the skills and abilities in creating therapeutic relationships, understanding process issues, working with feelings and staying with pain. That is our domain as counsellors, and that is what, in my belief, organizations desperately need today. We can do it because our counsellors are the best in the world. British counselling training and practice is the best there is: without apology we can accept that we lead the world in these areas. Counselling research, counselling theories, counselling gurus and, until recently, counselling writing—undoubtedly, other countries are better; but not in training and not in practice. Our training is comprehensive and integral, our practice is wide and excellent.

If as workplace counsellors we are to become relevant, integrated and part of organizations, we do need not to contort ourselves into becoming Organizational Development experts, HR or Personnel Directors, advisers to managers, etc. All we need to do is what we do best as counsellors and apply it to the organization as well as the individual client.

Issue 18 Autumn 1997

Spirituality in Organizations?

Michael Joseph and Maryjo Scrivani

Just as in the past, organizations were reluctant to acknowledge that employees had physical and emotional needs, the idea of their spirituality remains dormant. Perhaps that is now changing.

*T*he concept of 'spirituality' is being considered increasingly frequently as having relevance for organizations. In this introductory article, we seek to raise some of the issues and ask questions about the relevance of this topic for workplace counsellors and others who have a concern for the holistic welfare of staff. At this stage, we have deliberately omitted definitions, which can lead to protracted debate in themselves. Although there are many perspectives, we would maintain that human beings can be regarded as having four major dimensions: intellectual, physical, emotional and spiritual.

Organizations have long been prepared to assist staff in intellectual development, through education and training, to improve knowledge and skills. More recently they have seen the value of being proactive in staff development and are utilizing skill/knowledge development to facilitate progression planning, act as an incentive for staff retention and help balance the spread of skills as the organization grows.

Awareness of physical well-being is also widespread now. As we grow in our understanding of health issues, the need for exercise, preventive healthcare and stress reduction is common knowledge. Again, organizations are willing to assist employees in their quest for good physical health by arranging, for example, health screening, on-site yoga classes and even provision of gym facilities.

Enlightened organizations have begun taking steps to assist employees in attaining a level of emotional health, recognizing that we are whole persons: for our individual contribution to be at its best, we need to be in the optimum possible all-round health. In-house and external counselling services, EAPs and staff workshops, are just some of the approaches which are increasingly used to raise the quality of emotional health.

Lastly, we come to the spiritual dimension. 'There is no spirituality in organizations', one senior executive of a large multinational said to us recently. By and large, this would seem to be true. Perhaps more specifically, organizations are not yet at the stage where they are willing or able to acknowledge that spiritual development (transcending but not transgressing individual belief systems) might be both desirable and necessary in order to allow the whole person to function most completely and effectively in their place of work.

We would contend that it is through our spiritual side that we most easily re-evaluate our principles, and our connection to each other and the world around us. It is through awareness and connection with this aspect of ourselves that we find perhaps the greatest resources to enable us to fulfil our potential, working as a whole, integrated, and eventually inter-connected, person.

Doctoral research

We believe that it is not yet understood how deepening this last dimension, specifically within an organizational setting, might affect individuals and the life of an organization. We are currently undertaking doctoral research into this question. The purpose of this research is to attempt to understand: first, can we break the bonds of silence which stop us from speaking about spirituality and begin to reap the benefits from this less acknowledged part of ourselves? Secondly, if we can, how might individuals in organizations put aside their fears and differences to join together to develop their spiritual side? Lastly, what impact would that have on individuals and the organization if this were to happen? Our current view is that spirituality within an organization is manifest in the deep bond occurring when people share common values, principles and a sense of purpose greater than themselves. Think back through your own past and consider any groups to which you may have belonged, which worked together elegantly—surmounting obstacles and carried forward with an energy outside of individual members. The sense of the whole is greater than any individual's sense of self and the synergy between people in these situations is remarkable.

What are the implications for the workplace counsellor? Typically our training and practice enable us to recognize and work with emotional issues and we are well aware of the interaction of physical well-being on overall emotional health. Nothing, however, in training and little in current practice, gives any insight into the impact of lack of spiritual well-being or, indeed, on the positive side, how we might help clients achieve their full potential by developing or exploiting the spiritual part of themselves. If, as we have suggested earlier, it is this dimension which offers the greatest potential for motivation, satisfaction and growth, and is the gateway to the deepest resources we have, then surely this must be a major area of awareness and focus for the counsellor.

Issue 18 Autumn 1997

Working with Meditation

Ian Macwhinnie

All of us in the workplace must identify to an extent with our roles and job titles. Nevertheless, the essential core of our selves is beyond such limitation and calls for acknowledgement.

Nobody has yet been reported as saying on their deathbed that they wished they had spent more time at the office. Yet, however much we may enjoy our work, there are probably not many for whom this statement would not strike some resonating chord. There is within it an implication that, whatever our level of success and personal achievement through work, there may remain some aspect of ourselves that is not nourished through our working life and relationships. In addition, so much of our personal sense of self-esteem is tied up in our perceptions of work life: where we are on the corporate ladder, the way we are treated by our 'superiors', how much we earn. Any conflict or lack of satisfaction from these aspects quickly translates itself into feelings of unhappiness and lack of self-worth.

Many of us may feel caught in a double bind: we have to work, we have to define ourselves through our work roles, and yet we may not feel that work itself gives us the sense of fulfilment and identity we need at a deeper level of ourselves. What do we need to be able to do so that, on our deathbeds, there will be no regrets about how much time we spent at the office, or indeed, no regrets at all? To achieve this demands coming into connection with our sense of spirituality, the centre of our experience, so that a sense of our essential core remains even under the stressful experience of work.

One description of our spirituality, or one aspect of it, is that it is that something which persists over time. It remains constant in spite of changes that happen over the years physically, emotionally and psychologically. Meditation is a process whereby we can come back into contact, in increasing degrees over time, with this perennial aspect of ourselves, this part of ourselves which exists beyond our everyday, conscious thoughts, fears and feelings. It means that whatever may be happening in our work, or even in our personal lives, we have a way of getting in touch with that basic, original aspect of ourselves that remains essentially untroubled, like the eye at the centre of a typhoon.

To compare our lives to a three-legged stool: one leg reflects our daily, active working life (work), another our rest and recreation (r&r) which includes our personal life, family, hobbies and sleep. The third leg of the stool is our spirituality, which is as different from the other two as ice is different from the liquid and gaseous states of water. If we live our lives only using the work and r&r legs of the stool, we shall always be essentially unstable. Balance will be more of a wobbling. Perhaps many of us feel that our lives are like this, and the only way that balance can be maintained, like a bicycle on its two wheels, is when there is continuous motion. We lead 'driven' lives to stop us falling over! But if we are able to add that third leg to the stool, we will have a basic stability which is balanced whatever the circumstances. Just as when you pull one leg of a stool, all three move, it is possible to have an active outward-going work life, and still carry along the leg of spirituality as well.

Creating a balance

There are many and varied techniques of meditation designed to introduce our daily selves to those more perennial, fundamental aspects of ourselves. It is important to remember that these techniques are tools for accessing these deeper aspects of ourselves, they are not goals in themselves. We travel by car to reach a destination, but once there, the car is no longer required. Techniques help to take us behind our everyday thoughts, feelings and perceptions to that place where all these sensations arise. For example, when we feel happy, where does that happiness come from? Many different things can cause that bubble of happiness to arise: the warmth of the sun or watching a child at play, but happiness does not come from the objects or experiences themselves. The happiness we feel is triggered by these experiences, but the actual happiness comes from within.

Meditation is a process where we can contact this source within us directly and can come out of the experience more enriched, and with a sense of inner strength, which makes it easier to go through more trying times. The converts to a kind of 'spirituality' who, for example, chant 'om' to get parking spaces, are mistaking spiritual orientation for just another kind of competitive edge. What we are aiming for is, in fact, quite the opposite: it is to recognize that behind all the competition, behind all the natural injustice of the relationship between employer and employee, the differences in salary which measure people's relative worth—behind all this, we share something common and equal, which makes each of us special, without making anyone else less so.

To begin to see and experience this is to give our days a quality, whether at work or home, that may allow us, on our deathbeds, not to feel that we have somehow missed out. ◉

Issue 9 Summer 1995

Climbing out of the Crowded Closet

Lynn Macwhinnie

It is up to workplace counsellors to help companies instigate counselling services and to be proud of the benefits they bring to employees, as well as to their own public image.

The media have done much to bring the concept of counselling into the public arena and rarely a day goes by without it being mentioned in the press in one context or another. Its juxtaposition though is often related to a person's individual needs due to a traumatic incident. With the exception of public organizations such as the Police, Transport or Fire services, we do not hear a great deal about companies which have a counselling service available to their employees. Why is this? Whether through government NHS policies, Acts of Parliament or changing attitudes, organizations are increasingly having to pick up their share of the health care of the population which comes under their corporate roof. There are organizations such as The Boots Company which has a well established tradition of caring for the emotional health and welfare of all their employees both past and present. Mutual loyalty should not be such a rarity. Other corporates, however, have been somewhat slower off the mark and, in some cases, the new brooms of restructuring have swept away the company counselling provision.

Who influences whether the counselling service is actively promoted and readily utilized? Is it those looking at costs, or those who are fearful of any imagined negative perception of them or the company (i.e. you only have a counselling service if your company is in bad shape) or those who are just blinkered? Not uncommon are anecdotal tales of the disdainful attitude of senior management with their outright rejection of anything remotely connected to the seemingly 'soft' issues of emotions. Without doubt, the company culture, and the key players modelling that culture, play a major role in whether or not a counselling provision stays, or is even taken on board in the first place.

Yet while there are companies who make it well known, at least among their employees, that a confidential counselling service (internal or external) is available, there are other companies who take a more ambivalent view. While, on the face of things, the stigma surrounding counselling has gone, the message which is sent out to the employees is one of 'we care but don't want to know'. Counselling can only stay in the shadows, as indeed can the emotions it mirrors within the organization. Lip service may be given publicly to the fact there is a counselling provision but the employee's access to it can be littered with oblique obstacles and practical constraints.

It is also highly important that companies do not misguidedly believe they have an internal counselling service when a personnel or line manager returns from a counselling skills course. It does not confer the status of counsellor. There is a significant difference between therapeutic counselling and the use of counselling skills. One means of differentiation is that the former is a process and the latter is a tool. Attending the course may alert the employee to the distinction between the two, but far too often the company ignores such finer details and shows little inclination to be informed otherwise. After all, so the reasoning goes, why should the line manager/personnel officer/supervisor not be the company counsellor too? And no take-up of their services obviously indicates a lack of need on the part of the employees. Doesn't it?

With mistrust (often rising out of confusion) a prevailing sentiment amongst employers and employees, it is time all organizations took their role of employee support more seriously. They need to allow themselves to be better informed and be guided by those who know about counselling—the counsellors. Companies using a counselling service should speak out about the effectiveness of their provision, and that being at the cutting edge of employee support is not a sign of weakness. Quite the contrary.

There are external counselling providers who insist that they will only undertake a contract with a company if they are working publicly, and that the counselling service is not a hidden resource. There are others who do not make this a proviso—perhaps believing they can gradually influence a company to reconsider its position. The footnote to this is the perspective of the counsellor. How can we expect organizations to take us seriously if we are not prepared to demonstrate the positive effects of counselling? We have to be prepared to think systemically, be aware of how we influence the bottom line and learn to brief ourselves on the organizational system. The media has played a part in bringing counselling into the public arena and, as seems to be the general trend once a subject is fashionable, in shouting it down. Growth should not depend on the media or on organizations accepting *carte blanche* that we are useful. We must prove it, this is part of our responsibility. So maybe we all—workplace counsellors and organizations—need to climb out of the crowded closet. Then mutually beneficial relationships will become the norm for everyone making the commitment to counselling at work. ●

Issue 16 Spring 1997

ACW Membership

- Are you an in-house or external workplace counsellor?
- Are you a line manager, team leader or working in human resources?
- Do you use counselling skills in your work?
- Do you want to encourage a positive workplace culture?
- Are you interested in training as a workplace counsellor?
- Is your organization providing access to counselling services?
- Do you want to keep informed of developments in workplace counselling?

If you have answered YES to any of these questions, then individual or organizational membership of the Association for Counselling at Work (ACW) is for you.

What is ACW?

ACW is a well established specialist division of the British Association for Counselling (BAC). ACW promotes and supports the professional practice of counselling and the development of counselling skills in work-related settings. Members of ACW include organizations and individuals in the finance, commerce, industry, government, education and health sectors.

What can ACW do for me?

ACW membership provides:
- a forum and mutual support network
- news, views and articles in ACW's quarterly journal *Counselling at Work*
- professional and personal development opportunities:
- access to information, experience and resources relating to training, professional practice and implementation of counselling and counselling skills
- links to organizations in the industrial, commercial and service sectors; in the public and voluntary sectors and with other professional bodies

How do I join ACW?

Membership of ACW is open to individuals and organizations who are members of BAC, for an additional annual fee. **Individual membership is £25. Organizational membership is £60.**

Send your full contact details with a cheque payable to BAC, Membership Office, 1 Regent Place, Rugby CV21 2PJ, for the appropriate amount and include your membership number, if known. Alternatively, if you are not a current member of BAC, contact 01788 550899 and ask for a copy of their Invitation to Membership. If you have any queries, contact the ACW office on 01788 335617, or fax: 01788 335618.